how to heal a workplace

how to heal a workplace

Tackle Trauma, Foster Psychological Safety and Boost Happiness at Work

Kerry Howard

WILEY

First published in 2023 by John Wiley & Sons Australia, Ltd
Level 4, 600 Bourke St, Melbourne, Victoria 3000, Australia

Typeset in Garamond Premier Pro 12/15pt

© Ms Pink Enterprises Pty Ltd 2023

The moral rights of the author have been asserted

ISBN: 978-1-394-15447-0

A catalogue record for this book is available from the National Library of Australia

Cover design by Wiley
Cover and internal 'growth' image by © Olga Ubirailo/Getty Images
Author Photo: Wilomark Imagery

Disclaimer
The material in this publication is of the nature of general comment only, and does not represent professional advice. It is not intended to provide specific guidance for particular circumstances and it should not be relied on as the basis for any decision to take action or not take action on any matter which it covers. Readers should obtain professional advice where appropriate, before making any such decision. To the maximum extent permitted by law, the author and publisher disclaim all responsibility and liability to any person, arising directly or indirectly from any person taking or not taking action based on the information in this publication.

Contents

Introduction

As human beings, we spend the majority of our waking adult life at work. Depending on the country that you reside in, your working hours may vary, but even in the most balanced societies, we spend more than one-third of our life at work.

Given that we spend so much time in this environment and our occupation is often a key component to our sense of identity and self-worth, it is essential to our overall functioning in life to be able to operate in a supportive environment. This means a workplace that provides psychological safety and security and affords us a positive sense of our value and contribution. It means a workplace that gives us an opportunity to meet our greatest emotional need: the need for connection.

The global way of working is rapidly changing, and workplaces have devolved and decentralised, fuelled by the COVID-19 pandemic. Prior to the pandemic we were seeing this trend in decentralisation, particularly in knowledge industries where a computer and internet access were all employees needed to deliver outcomes. For multinational corporations with employees located in different countries around the world, it posed unique challenges that often required dedicated human resources (HR) teams to ensure worker safety and protect employers from potential legal claims spanning multiple cultures and jurisdictions.

It is rare to find a true multinational corporation that has been able to navigate the competing nuances of culture and expectations to create a truly satisfied, efficient and effective workforce.

There are exceptions, most of them in the technology space (LinkedIn, Google, SpaceX). Reports of high levels of staff satisfaction imply the workplace is a happy and productive one. This may be a reflection on the types of people who are drawn to work in these environments. In the technology field we see high levels of neurodiversity, which brings with it a greater cognitive flexibility and potentially higher tolerance of difference. In the HR field, we see more people who have high levels of emotional intelligence and are, therefore, also more likely to have a higher tolerance for diversity. So, what does that say about other workplaces and occupations?

Embracing difference in the work environment is something that is written into many workplace codes of conduct, but is rarely truly embraced in application. Group dynamics come into play, and many conservative workplaces appreciate diversity, as long as it's packaged in a dark suit and white shirt. Yet every workplace requires a variety of personality types to ensure its people can innovate and find creative solutions to complex challenges.

Difference can be expressed through personality, but it can also be created by action. When a member of the team acts in a way that seems to expose the team to scrutiny, it is not uncommon for the renegade member of the team to be excluded while the rest of the team band together to protect themselves from further ridicule. Psychological constructs around group membership often facilitate this type of behaviour in workplaces, but it can have a significant negative impact on the person who raised the alarm.

How we manage and treat our people at work can be directly linked to managing psychological safety at work. Another example is the type of work that our occupation exposes us to. We know that public safety workers (defence, emergency services, hospital staff) are routinely exposed to traumatic incidents as a direct result of the type of work that they do. In our society we recognise that the incidence of post-traumatic stress disorder (PTSD) can be disproportionately higher in these sectors than in other industries.

Then there are the sectors exposed to occupational violence, and, surprisingly, these are often the 'helping' professions: ambulance officers, nurses and, perhaps unexpectedly, teachers. Ambulance officers and nurses are often on the front line when people are in trouble, potentially under the influence of illicit substances or alcohol, which can expose them to negative behaviours. As occupational groups, the 'helping' professions can be significantly impacted by these types of incidents, because the nature of the work tends to attract quite empathic people. It can be hard to fathom why you would be hurt while trying to help someone — quite a different psychological position than those in the armed services, for example.

To most people's surprise, we see that teachers are significantly impacted by violence in schools. The rates of workers compensation claims by teachers for occupational violence is almost as high as emergency services workers.[1] For similar reasons to our medical personnel, teaching generally attracts a more empathic and caring personality, and like anyone who is exposed to violence they also struggle with these incidents.

There are multiple ways that people may feel unsafe or disempowered in the workplace. My aim in this book is to help you understand why these situations occur, and provide clear guidance as to what you can do to support your people to tackle trauma and foster psychological safety. By taking a proactive approach to the challenges that can arise in the workplace, you will improve the culture of your workplace, be it large or small. Ensuring your people feel valued and supported by their employer will lead to increased satisfaction and boost the general feeling of happiness at work.

Part I
Workplace Culture

CHAPTER 1

What is workplace culture?

Why it's the key to profitability

I am often asked why I focus on trying to help organisations change their culture, and I point out that we spend the majority of our waking adult life at work. If we are constantly exposed to a toxic workplace culture, the chances of us being able to operate at our best and live our lives 'full of awesome' is pretty slim.

Conversely, if employees are experiencing mental health issues, for example, then their behaviour in the workplace is not going to be balanced or reasonable at all times. When employees feel safe enough to share their mental health issues, we can provide support for that team member. However we all experience difficulties in life, and we often don't recognise that they impact our mental health, and we don't label them as such.

I am sure that, like me, you have grown up in a world that told you that you needed to maintain a separation between work and life — don't let your personal problems cross over into your working life, and vice versa — but it's not only unreasonable to expect this type of compartmentalisation, it's damn near impossible to achieve!

As human beings we have many complex feelings and emotional experiences that impact our mood; we are not robots. We cannot merely switch ourselves into 'work mode' and switch off the fact that we are having relationship problems, or our parents or child are sick. There are many occupations where it can feel like we readily switch into 'work mode'. We see this in occupations that require uniforms; we put on the uniform and our behaviour changes, but it doesn't mean that the stress of our home life stops affecting us.

The same is true in reverse: our experiences at work can spill over into our mood and behaviour at home. When we are unhappy at work, it places pressure on our home life. Whether it's financial pressure, time pressure or other excessive work expectations, it is impossible to separate the impact of our working and home lives — and unreasonable of us to expect that they can be separated!

The one constant reflection that I hear from staff who have had a difficult time, but managed to work through it, is that they had a supportive supervisor. The perception of 'support' changes depending on the workplace, but it is essentially where the staff member felt that their challenges in life were seen by their supervisor to be a temporary glitch in their work performance, and they were provided the space to get through the challenge and get on with life, without it affecting their working life.

In essence, their situation was appropriately viewed as 'temporary' and they were trusted to get back to full capacity as soon as practicable. The important element here is 'trust'.

What is workplace culture?

Many people believe that they know what the term 'workplace culture' means, but for clarity, I am going to define it here and explain what it looks like in practicality. Workplace culture is the environment that you create for your employees. It plays a powerful role in determining their satisfaction with their career, their interpersonal relationships and their career progression. The culture of your workplace is determined by a combination of the company's leadership and the employees' values, beliefs and attitudes, which translate into behaviours and interactions that contribute to the relational environment of your workplace. In general, these are the intrinsic rules that govern interpersonal connections in the workplace between peers.

Workplace culture should align with the company's mission and vision statements, and be supported by policies and procedures that are designed to ensure the workplace functions effectively and achieves its overall goals. However, when I am called into an organisation to support cultural change, the number one problem is that the workplace culture has veered off track and is no longer aligned with the mission or vision.

Workplace culture can be strongly impacted by the leadership, and we often see issues develop in the culture when there is a misalignment between the leader, the company's mission and vision, and the staff. There can be several reasons for this misalignment, but not addressing the misalignment is a sure-fire way to create a toxic workplace culture.

Workplace culture is the environment that you create for your employees

---

Toxic workplace culture

We have all heard the term 'toxic culture' thrown around, but I will outline what I mean by this term. Toxicity in the workplace develops from a pattern of combined behaviours that are counterproductive. When promoted by toxic leadership, a toxic culture incorporates six specific behaviours:

- passive hostility
- shaming

- indifference

- team sabotage

- negativity

- exploitation.[2]

Toxic cultures are known to promote attitudes that adversely impact employee psychological wellbeing (see figure 1.1). Psychological wellbeing is also defined by six attributes:

- autonomy

- environment management

- personal growth

- positive relationships

- having life goals

- self-acceptance.[3]

Figure 1.1: The impact of toxic cultures on employee psychological wellbeing

In one particular study that considered the impact of a toxic workplace culture on psychological wellbeing, it determined, not surprisingly, that wellbeing is lower in employees who are exposed to toxic workplace cultures. What might be surprising is that almost 80 per cent of workplaces met the criteria for toxicity![3]

The researchers identified that there are three main strategies adopted by employees who are confronted with these toxic work environments:

- **Active rejection:** These employees are the whistle-blowers, the fighters against injustice, who take action against the toxicity of the workplace and see quitting as the last resort. These employees represent over one-third of the workforce, and you will read some of their stories in this book.

- **Passive rejection:** These employees are those who tend to hide their dissatisfaction from the perpetrators (usually the leadership) while sharing their dissatisfaction with their peers. These employees represent a staggering 40 per cent of the workforce and perceive that *all* workplaces are toxic, so they remain passively disengaged because they are pessimistic. They believe that it is better the devil you know, than the devil you don't!

- **Escapees:** These are the ones who decide that it is easier to get out as quickly as possible, in some cases leaving the professional field. These employees represent the remaining 27 per cent of the workforce and often react swiftly to toxic experiences of blatant harassment, threats and intimidation.

Employees with higher levels of psychological wellbeing are more likely to escape when the organisation toxicity worsens, whereas employees with the lowest psychological wellbeing are the most likely to become passive rejectors.[4]

It isn't that difficult to see why these numbers need our attention. If 80 per cent of workplaces have a moderate to high toxicity, and

40 per cent of those employees are passively disengaged, 33 per cent are actively disrupting the workplace and 27 per cent are actively looking for work elsewhere, then it really isn't hard to understand why actively leading to reduce toxicity in the workplace should be the major goal of all compassionate leaders. The disenfranchisement of our human resources is leading to significantly reduced productivity, and this is silently eroding the profitability of businesses globally.

The Great Resignation

> **The Great Resignation:** The mass exodus from the work environment observed post-pandemic. The term was coined by Anthony Klotz, a professor of management at University College London's School of Management, in May 2021.

The phenomena of the Great Resignation was first observed in 2021 following the disruption to the way that we work thanks to the pandemic. In July 2021, a Gallup Poll revealed that almost half the American working population was actively looking for new roles. Business is facing a staggeringly high resignation rate and record numbers of unfilled positions.[5] The United States quit rate is at its highest in over 20 years, hovering at almost 3 per cent since early 2021.[6]

> **Quit rate:** The number of employees who voluntarily resign, as opposed to as the result of redundancy or being fired.

There are several reasons for this phenomenon, but the primary reason is that the impact of the pandemic on people's freedom meant that their discontent with life was linked with the employer that they were connected with at the time of the strongest lockdowns and control over their movements in society.

In Australia, we saw less of this movement until 2022, primarily due to the prolonged lockdowns, which affected our general sense of security and limited the number of people changing roles due to the need for stable employment. The Australian Bureau of Statistics' annual job mobility survey shows that Australians are on the move at their highest rate in over a decade: 9.5 per cent in 2022, up 2 per cent from 2021. Not surprisingly, the highest change was seen in Victoria, usually a reasonably stable state in terms of job mobility. As the state that experienced the most prolonged lockdowns around the pandemic, it went from 7.2 per cent in 2021 to a whopping 10.1 per cent in 2022.[7]

In other countries like the United Kingdom, the statistics around economic inactivity give a clearer picture about the impact of the pandemic on the labour market. Since the start of 2021, there have been some alarming changes around economic inactivity (people who are not actively engaged in the workforce due to ill health, retirement, study, etc), despite an overall decline in the total number from 411 863 to 378 073, which on the surface would appear to be good news, certainly that is how the UK Government is espousing these numbers. However, when we dig into the data, we see some significant and alarming trends.[8]

What the data is telling us and how it affects your business

From the beginning of 2021 until May 2022 in the UK, we see sickness rates are out of control: temporary sick rates showed a 740 per cent increase from 3648 to 30 640, and long-term sick rates more than tripled from 67 487 to 208 655. At the same time, fewer people are studying, with student numbers declining by two-thirds — from 339 380 down to 139 690 — and more people are retiring, with rates skyrocketing from 6851 to 63 174 — a 1022 per cent increase! Although the overall trend now looks like it's improving, there are much higher numbers of people who are unable to participate in the workforce due to health concerns, and many who are opting out of the labour market and retiring early.

The only real positive is in the number of discouraged workers, those who were not looking for work because they believed that no jobs were available — the number declined massively from 57 158 to 21 958, an incredible 138 per cent decrease!

So what does all this labour market data actually have to do with your business? Everything! Recruitment specialists are talking about the fact that it is now an employee's market, at a time when many industries are struggling with the skills gap between the available prospects and the requirements of the role. One of the biggest challenges with fewer people studying is that we already have a skills shortage. Recruitment has become much more of a 'take what's available' for the employer, leading to some significant challenges in an under-skilled labour market with unrealistic expectations of its worth.

Employees are seeking roles with employers that offer them more wellbeing support and greater flexibility than ever before. There are several reasons why we ended up in this situation, but realistically, the labour market has been decimated by the departure of the Baby Boomers, many of whom retired through the pandemic, leaving a major skills shortage in the market. Most organisations are now led by Gen X (born 1965–1980), with Gen Y/Millennials (born 1981–1996) and Gen Z/iGen/Zoomers (1997–2012) the main players in the workforce.

It's an employee market and they want greater support for mental health and real balance between home and work

---

What does our generation have to do with our work ethic?

In Western societies, our 'generation' defines many things about our psychological and social dimensions, and is expressed in commonly held beliefs or views of the world that are shaped by the social experiences of each generation. There are two overlapping theories about how generations form. The 'pulse-rate hypothesis' gives rise to the naming conventions and timeframes that we are most familiar with, and essentially claims that each generation develops a particular 'peer personality' based on the time period in which each one reaches adulthood.[9] Social scientists follow the 'imprint hypothesis' of generations, which indicates that the specific historical events that are experienced during our early lives shape our outlook on the world and differentiate us from our parents.[10]

In broad terms, our current society and, by default, our workplaces are influenced by the current 'living' cohorts who are still participating in the labour market: Baby Boomers, Gen X, Gen Y and Gen Z. In terms of population numbers, the Baby Boomers were the largest generational cohort until they gave birth to Gen Y. Most Baby Boomers are in or looking at retirement, so the majority of modern workplaces are filled with members of Gen X, Gen Y and Gen Z. We need to actively manage the expectations of Gen Z and prepare for the influx of Gen Alpha in the next five years.

Baby Boomers

Most Baby Boomers were raised by parents whose lives had been impacted by the Great Depression. As such, they were often raised with austerity, and subject to strict rules and social obligations until the emergence of the 1960s counterculture. These varied experiences really affected how they parented Gen Y. There was a significant increase in expectations of university education, and corresponding expectations around success in the occupational sphere.

As workers, Baby Boomer males align with a strong work ethic: diligence and dedication to an employer; most of their careers were spent with a single employer. Baby Boomer females tended to work outside the home to bring in additional income once children were at school and society allowed it. In the 1960s, many young Baby Boomer women were forced to quit their jobs once they married. As such, Gen Y was raised by a generation of mothers who stayed home until they went to school, and then engaged in the workforce, often part time, usually to be able to provide more for their children.

Generation X

Gen X is the generation that saw mothers entering the workforce in a time before the advent of formalised childcare or after-school care. Higher rates of divorce meant that this was the first generation that experienced high levels of sole parenting, and this was usually done by the mother. They learned how to fend for themselves because they had to; so they learned to solve problems. As a result, they were open to thinking outside the box.

The 80s saw the rise of music videos and subcultures develop around punk, metal and goth. They were exposed to widespread health concerns with AIDS, were the first generation to engage with technology and were more likely to get a university degree than previous generations. Gen X women believed that they could have a career and a family and sacrificed a lot to achieve both.

They embraced individualism and are known for being entrepreneurial and productive in the workplace. They are committed to their profession, not necessarily the employer, and they look to change career focus every ten years or so. They tend to get on with things because they were raised to be self-sufficient.

Generation Y

The social changes that impacted the Baby Boomers through the 1960s really shaped how they would parent their offspring. As a result, Gen Y were raised to believe that they could achieve anything they set their mind to — that success was theirs for the taking, they just had to ask for it. As their mothers self-sacrificed to give them more, Gen Y started to develop more egocentricity than earlier generations as they were given a lot of support from their parents, coupled with a lot of expectation.

This generation saw the movement from personal computing to mobile technology, and the emergence of new technologies and social media through their teen years, which further enhanced their egocentricity. They are known for being ambitious and expect to rise rapidly up the corporate ladder, while also expecting a reasonable work-life balance. Gen Y was the first generation to expect that they could have it all, and that they should be supported to do so by their parents and their employers.

Gen Y are creative and bring a stronger entrepreneurial focus to the workplace than Gen X — this is the generation that has created the notion of the digital nomad. They seek adventure and success — so in the workplace they thrive on creative and reactive work environments.

> **Digital nomad:** A person who works online in various locations while travelling, rather than in one fixed location.

Generation Z

As parents, Gen X were more inclined to encourage their children to be self-sufficient, but they were also more aware of the dangers in society, so they have tended to be more over-protective of their Gen Z children. Gen Z are the first generation recognised as true digital natives due to their access to portable electronic devices, and have been identified as 'technoholics'.

Gen Z grew up without a lot of adult supervision, similar to their parents, but they had more access to digital entertainment, so they didn't play outside as much. They weren't allowed to get around on their own due to 'stranger danger', and they didn't engage in risky play, so they struggle with assessing risk and problem-solving.

Gen Z were afforded more awareness and acceptance of mental health challenges, and their parents were often too busy working to effectively manage these challenges with their children. Due to their digital exposure, Gen Z are the most egocentric generation we have seen so far, defining their self-worth by their social media likes, resulting in poorer self-perception. This generation has a declining attention span and, arguably, their IQ is falling. In humans, an IQ test is designed to assess several abilities — reasoning, problem-solving, perception of relationships between things and the storage and retrieval of information. As they are no longer required to read and retain information, the development of Gen Z's other abilities will be impaired.

Gen Z were also raised in a school system that tried to level the playing field by not grading students against each other; rather they sought to grade students on their own merit. As a result, this generation didn't develop resilience around failure. Their exposure to digital products established a dopamine source that has fuelled their brains from adolescence, as a result they prefer to relax by zoning out watching movies or social media and engage socially by gaming online with friends they have never actually met. This new digital social world has proven to be beneficial in the absence of real-world peer connections, but we have to ask if they had spent more time in the outside world as children, whether this need would have been met through actual friendships.

The next generation are currently beginning their adolescence and the experiences of Gen Z are set to be magnified in Gen Alpha. Gen Z is a young workforce that struggles with focus and attention, can't solve problems, has a strong understanding of mental health and awareness of their rights, but little resilience, neatly wrapped up in extreme egocentricity. This means that we have about five years to resolve these challenges before the next generation of young adults enters the workforce. Ironically, it is the Gen X leaders who will finally have to parent their children in the workforce.

It's not all bad, the creativity and diversification that has developed over the past 60 years has not only changed the way we work across society, but also how we parent and live.

Where to from here?

The implications of industrialisation have meant that as machinery and technology improved, the nature of our work as humans has changed from predominantly physical labour to knowledge labour — completely changing the nature of our workplaces. The changing nature of our society has changed the way we eat, socialise and raise families. The pandemic has really narrowed the focus of these changes and given rise to the reality that most knowledge workers can work from anywhere with a laptop and an internet connection. That doesn't necessarily mean that working this way is good for us socially, but it is the reality of what 'can' be done.

Time-poor Gen X parents are now having to manage the results of their parenting approach in their Gen Z staff: teaching them problem-solving skills, how to assess risks and providing meaningful work that is 'exciting' enough to keep them from becoming disengaged. As a generation, Gen Z can focus more on problems and struggle with solutions because their time-poor parents fixed all their problems for them. They can lack motivation for things that don't serve their own needs and they often struggle to take initiative.

Now, I know I am making broad, sweeping statements here that many might disagree with or be offended by. Rather than seeking to be overly negative, I believe that it is important that leaders understand the societal challenges that we have to manage in the modern workplace because these challenges in managing staff are widespread and cross-cultural.

I am also speaking about myself here as a Gen X parent with Gen Z children and staff. Although I appreciate their knowledge of technology and their adaptability to change, at times I feel like a parent in the workplace, and that can be as frustrating as when I was actually parenting adolescents.

I was also a sole parent who was incredibly supportive of my children around their mental health. I raised them to value money and have a good work ethic, but I continued to support them financially in one form or another until they completed their studies and started working full time, which has only happened recently. My children are both in their late 20s and I have been paying for their private health insurance and medical expenses — although they are on notice that this will stop once they are established with their full-time income.

Why did I do it? A combination of means and awareness of the importance of good health and education is probably behind this approach. They have worked part time to support themselves around studies and their education was important to me, so I felt it was important to support their health needs. However, I have other friends who have allowed their children to remain at home and disengaged from the world, while they supported them financially because their children struggled with resilience. We have spent their whole lives trying to protect them from the big, bad world and created a generation whose fallback is learned helplessness.

The intergenerational changes in our industrialised world have given rise to a broad variety of expectations in our people. Many workplace cultures have become toxic in the wake of the growing egocentricity of Gen Y and Gen Z. Don't get me wrong, Boomers and Gen X had their fair share of big egos, but they were more scattered across society and based on the social tenets of success.

The internet has given rise to social media and online gaming, and provided the perception that what I say or do is seen by many people and they are all interested in it. It's a one-way communication medium with few feedback loops, with the exception of likes or followers. This has given rise to the notion of 'fame' for no real reason except that people are watching. That is why the number one career goal of Gen Z and Gen Alpha is to become an 'influencer'. They honestly believe that the world is interested in their opinion and their lives, so much so that their mood can be altered by the changing number of likes they have on Instagram. We have to understand their unrealistic expectations because we have to learn to help them adapt to keep them engaged in our workplace.

The challenge of building focus and resilience

There are multiple examples from organisations that I have worked with in the past couple of years that highlight the issue with this lack of resilience in Gen Z and the over-protective parenting of Gen X. A plumbing company I worked with were having a lot of difficulty with retaining apprentices — at the first hurdle of having to push themselves through a problem, the young person would often walk off the job and never return.

One story that stands out in my mind was about a plumber who was responsible for installing 200 toilets on a large construction job. His reasonably new apprentice was going to help and what better time to start than with 200 toilets to practice on. So the plumber demonstrates the first toilet, he demonstrates again with the second toilet but asks the apprentice to get more hands on. The apprentice takes the lead with the third toilet with the plumber supporting them. By the fourth toilet, the apprentice is installing it under instruction from the plumber — the first four toilets have taken them two hours to complete. The plumber leaves the apprentice to install them himself with instructions to come and ask if he has any concerns.

The plumber heads off to install another toilet and comes back when he is finished to check in on the apprentice. He is slow, but progressing, and so the plumber gets on with installing a couple more toilets before checking back in — the apprentice is having lunch. After lunch, the plumber checks in with the apprentice once he has finished toilet number five. It looks pretty good. It took him three hours, but the plumber reassures him that he will get faster. The plumber goes and installs another four toilets and it's the end of the day. The plumber returns to find the apprentice on his phone; toilet number six hasn't been started. When questioned, the apprentice said that he can't remember how to do it. The plumber tries to reassure him that he will show him again in the morning. The apprentice says that his Mum is coming to pick him up.

The plumber proceeds to go and collect his tools and packs up for the day, and as he is about to leave, the apprentice's Mum turns up and confronts the plumber about the fact that he is placing too much pressure on her son to perform and he won't be returning to the job. She quit for him! I wish this was a rare event, but with Gen X parents it is common.

Mindfully parenting through the challenges

I am a Gen X parent, but I believe I have a bit more awareness of these generational challenges. As my children have grown older, I take the time to teach them how to speak up for themselves, even when I want to step in and fight for them. Modern parents have been so influenced by the 'rights'

17

of the individual to be treated with respect and with fairness that when we anticipate a level of unfairness, we jump in to protect them a little too often — as a result, these children haven't developed resilience.

I recall when my eldest daughter was working her first part-time job in a local café about ten years ago. One evening as I'm waiting to pick her up (because we would never let them walk home, ride their bike or catch public transport after dark), I see the café owner yelling at my daughter about something she hadn't done. I watch 'bemused' as my daughter scurries off to complete the task before finishing up for the night. The owner approached me and asked me why I allowed her to yell at my daughter and not say anything. I said 'Are you paying her to do a job?' She said *Yes*. 'Is she doing it?' She said *No*. 'Have you asked her several times to do it?' She said *Yes*. I said, 'Welcome to my world! If she doesn't like it, she can quit. But your expression of frustration is reasonable to her because she knows that she didn't do what you asked. If you were being unreasonable, then she would have quit already!'

I was observing the same lack of focus in my daughter at work that I was seeing at home, after all — she was an adolescent! I was also very aware that her boss was frustrated by her lack of attention in much the same way that I was at home, so I had empathy for the boss's position. I had faith that my daughter would take action if it was ongoing and unreasonable — but she loved that job and they loved her. She worked there right through university until she moved away for further studies and our family are still warmly welcomed in that café, even ten years later.

No matter what industry you are in, the lack of resilience and focus in your younger team members can be a point of frustration. Many of you may have already had similar experiences with the Gen X parent of your Gen Z employees. They are a very protective generation of parents who have created such great dependency in their children that they will run away from a challenge, rather than pushing themselves to improve. As Gen X leaders, we now have to correct the over-protective parenting that has initiated learned helplessness in our Gen Z employees. Let's face it — we have to resolve the issues we created as parents by applying these parenting skills with our employees.

Adapting for a new generation: Why it is essential for growth

Awareness of the challenges is obviously only one of the issues that we must overcome. This generation is so sensitive to rejection that we often don't get an opportunity to support them to improve their problem-solving skills before they go off on stress leave or quit. Some large corporates have just accepted that high turnover is part of the industry. This is particularly noticeable in the fast-food industry, which has a strong reliance on young labour to maintain its business.

In the absence of finding better ways to improve retention, we have just accepted that the cost of business has increased. The bottom line isn't looking great, but for many large corporations, they feel relieved that they have been able to stay in business over the pandemic, so the reduced profitability has been accepted. However, as we begin to emerge from this, we have to face the reality that business has changed forever.

The post-pandemic world of business looks nothing like the corporate world of the past

---

The pandemic raised the profile of mental health in the world like never before. We have all been affected, and it has been completely normalised in society that the impact of events that are outside of our control will impact our mental health, but society is still looking to the health profession to fix the problem. There are not enough mental health professionals to fix the problem, and we need to find ways to support each other to help ourselves.

We need to understand mental health and wellbeing generally and apply it across our business. We don't have the time to wait for the staff member to get access to external support; it takes months to get an appointment with a psychologist or counsellor, and even then, the process of recovery is slow.

We have increased our mental health awareness across society, but what we haven't yet done is built an empowerment model of mental health. This model recognises the challenges that people can experience when under stress and assists us to build significantly more empathy for the position of our colleagues, rather than maintaining our egocentricity. This is really challenging to do when we have several generations in the workforce who have been raised to believe that they have 'rights' and 'needs', and what comes with that is a complete lack of insight and awareness that we need to interact as a member of a community.

As a result, the workforce now has to teach people to work more effectively as a team, how to be more inter-dependent, because society raised them to be self-absorbed and egocentric and then we overlaid the trappings of success, to create an unrealistic sense of value and influence leading to success. We see more examples of narcissistic behaviours in many areas of work, false egos built on the back of the outward demonstration of success. These tendencies have been honed in Gen Y by their Boomer parents — the need for the big house, great car, white picket fence and kids in private school. The evidence of success demonstrated by the 'labels', creating a consumer-driven society that thrives on dopamine bursts fuelled by external validation received from a variety of areas, but primarily social media. The pandemic actually increased our focus on electronic interactions in the absence of actual human connections.

The evidence of success demonstrated by the 'labels', creating a consumer driven society that thrives on dopamine bursts fuelled by external validation

---

We have to make plans to improve the resilience of our workforce, help them to grow skills in problem-solving, and encourage them to use their creativity to take initiative in the workplace. They are good people who need to be managed with patience and clear guidance. Understanding the intergenerational challenges will help you as a leader understand why the frustrations are there, and hopefully help you see that it is not just one or two challenging personalities. These are issues that are present in all workplaces around the globe.

It's a societal problem that we need to try and improve by raising global consciousness of the unintended consequences of digitisation. Rather than trying to turn back the clock and convert people to technophobia, we need to recognise the challenges that these changes have had on humans through the generations — both in our society and in the workplace.

Recruitment specialist spells out the future for business

Gill has been in recruitment for 20 years. She fell into recruitment in the medical field as a junior, but she had great people skills and very quickly worked her way up to become a senior HR leader in the organisation. She moved between short-term contracts and then into agency recruitment. Gill had always wanted to establish her own business and just as we entered the pandemic in early 2020, she launched Clover Lane Consulting.

Her business has been incredibly successful, and she built it up quickly, establishing a great name for herself as a very 'hands on' recruiter. Gill didn't want to follow the traditional recruitment model — she established the 'Recruitment Revolution', as she recognised that the old 'sales pitch' model of recruitment wasn't going to work in a post-COVID world. She has established herself as a disruptor in the recruitment space because of how she engages with her clients and their people.

You can't build a great business unless you have the right people. Gill had a few key approaches for how she built high-performing teams, such as never asking someone to do something that she wouldn't do herself. Gill is a compassionate leader, regardless of whether she is managing an individual or a team, and she believes that understanding 'softer skills' is really important in managing people.

> **Soft skills:** Personal attributes, such as creative thinking and problem solving, that contribute to success in the workplace.

Gill acknowledges that she is a coaching-focused leader, and she prides herself on her honesty in business. She is open with her clients in what the current 'employee market' means, that they may be giving her a task that isn't able to be delivered. That's the reality of our new post-pandemic employment landscape, not any personal failing.

As a leader, Gill believes in giving her people their autonomy and flexibility. She has always been a leader who believes in delegating the deliverable, and not clock-watching attendance. She really despises micro-managing and believes that empowering people to deliver and grow with purpose is the key to change, and essential in a decentralised workplace. This openness and acceptance really help to create buy-in with people.

Gill is very open about her mental health experiences. She has herself experienced workplace bullying and harassment at the hands of her general manager. Gill was very young, and she felt very isolated by this situation, but she used the opportunity to examine it from a distance — almost like an experiment. Gill stayed in this organisation for three years and, even though it was a challenging time, she kept turning up every day with a smile plastered on her face and going home every night and crying tears of frustration. She used to spend her time 'pretending' she was okay and believing that everyone else's life was great because they were all wearing their 'work mask', yet they were probably all suffering in a similar way to how she was.

Gill was able to use this negative experience to drive her focus on great people management. Gill didn't ever want to see anyone else experiencing the type of behaviour that she experienced at the hands of her general manager. This experience really moulded her approach to recruitment, ensuring that she is placing candidates in a 'safe' work environment.

How wellbeing at work starts with mental health

Gill now works with businesses where she mentors and coaches them in how to grow their business, resource with the right people, and lead with clarity and purpose. Gill hosts a podcast and sees herself as a workplace advocate; she is very passionate about equality, equity and leading in the right way.

Wellbeing at work is not about just going on a course or running a program, and Gill's view is that it is about having an ongoing, dedicated strategy for wellbeing at work. When she works with her business clients, she first spends time examining the culture. From the top of the leadership team, down to the newest cadet, it's the shared mindset that everyone has challenges in life, every single person has mental health, and we need to manage it.

It's time to create a dedicated strategy for mental health and wellbeing in your workplace

---

Gill believes that it is essential to understand the culture of her client organisations before she recruits for them. There have been businesses that she has decided she can't work with because they are not willing to examine their culture. It has cost her some work opportunities over time, but she is committed to the candidates she recruits to ensure that they are offered a safe place to work. Gill believes that her role is to help organisations learn how to engage and retain staff. She maintains an ongoing relationship with her client agencies that extends past the recruitment process and into mentoring great management skills into their organisations. She believes that building rapport between managers and new recruits creates safe psychological spaces for people to be open and communicate better.

Promoting the 'right' leaders

I asked Gill about the propensity for people to be promoted based on their technical skills without understanding that they need some people skills too. I also suggested that maybe we think about it in the wrong way, in the sense that a team leader who manages people for their technical expertise doesn't necessarily also have to do the people management.

Gill agrees that this is a huge problem in all sectors, and that people management is a completely different role. Whether in recruitment or the public sector, doing the job is different to managing people to do the job. We both agree that that this is where many businesses go wrong.

Technical experts are great at the job, but that's very different to managing others to do the job

---

There is a recognition that many businesses develop toxic cultures. Gill believes that this is a failure of the process of business development; the manager doesn't have the people skills or the awareness that they need to manage human resources. They haven't been mentored, trained, or coached in how to do that effectively.

From her recruitment background, Gill is aware that often people get promoted to management thinking it will be a better role, and then it doesn't meet expectations because of the different focus on managing the people rather than the work. Many people don't enjoy that. There needs to be better preparation in business to help people learn that management is a very people-oriented role that requires empathy and good communication, not just great process management skill.

Gill believes that emotional intelligence (EQ) is an undervalued leadership trait. I would agree wholeheartedly. A person's EQ doesn't get enough focus or attention when we are looking to grow our next generation of leaders.

> **EQ (emotional intelligence):** The ability to recognise, understand and manage our own and other people's emotions.

The workplace injury pandemic

I asked Gill about her experience with injured workers, given her business mentoring role. Research from SafeWork Australia suggests that the average time it takes someone to recover from a workplace incident is extensive, especially with psychological injuries where it takes almost two years to recover — at a minimum. Some people say that they never recover.

Gill believes workplace injuries are a pandemic in themselves; however, trying to measure that effect is very difficult. Gill believes that it's not easy to talk about, hard to prove and very challenging to resolve. She believes that the only way forward is to bring it to the fore of our community consciousness, and have more discussions like we are having in this book. Gill also believes that, while we should not diminish physical injuries, psychological injuries can be so much more debilitating. We can't see mental health challenges, and many people put on a brave face. She also sees that, in some workplaces, it's perceived as drama or not productive to talk openly about challenges, and that can only exacerbate the problems.

On a positive note, Gill believes that the pandemic has created more opportunities to be open and discuss challenges around mental health, and that has helped. She has seen some great progress in terms of it being okay to not be okay at work. This appears to be changing the face of employment entitlements and companies are now addressing that. Rather than providing benefits around company cars and bonuses, they are offering benefits around mental health and wellness programs. That can only be a good thing.

Gill believes that mental health and wellbeing needs to be looked at holistically, and it starts from the top. Rather than just having a mental health champion, or a mental health first aid team or mental health week or day, she believes that, in the future, there will be a conscious 'HR and Wellbeing' focus, where open dialogue and compassion is at the forefront. From a recruitment perspective, we are seeing the shift post-pandemic. Unless businesses can demonstrate great compassion and a focus on wellbeing, people are choosing not to work for them.

If your business isn't focused on supporting your people, they will move to an employer who does

---

How do we fix it?

We really need to take a pragmatic approach when making significant changes in how we engage staff, from recruitment through to ongoing wellbeing checks. As you work your way through this book, you will see that I offer many options for providing clarity around the expectations that we have of our people. By providing them with a clear and consistent framework around how we manage wellbeing in the workplace, we will support them to develop more adaptive ways of working, build resilience and improve their problem-solving skills, in turn improving employee engagement and, ultimately, increasing productivity.

By focusing on the key components of tackling trauma and promoting psychological safety, you are going to create an exceptional workplace culture for your people, increasing profits and creating a level of positivity that will translate into widespread happiness at work.

The first thing we need to understand is whether or not your current workplace is actually showing signs of toxicity. Please head over to my website to complete the 'Toxic Workplace Assessment' — this will provide you with a scorecard result that will help you to understand just how much work you may need to do to heal your workplace.

Please visit https://kerryannhoward.com/toxic-workplace-assessment/ to take the quiz

CHAPTER 2

Why it's really about collective mental health

The ability to maintain a separation between life and work is actually impossible to achieve. As we spend so much of our time engaged with our work (even if we spend less time in the actual physical workplace post-pandemic), the working environment will affect our personal life and vice versa.

I have already outlined how a toxic workplace culture can create challenges for the people who work in it by engendering a level of disengagement. It's important to recognise that each individual member of the team can also be experiencing challenges in their personal lives, and that can also impact how the workplace culture operates.

This is something that many of us will have observed at some point over our working lives — how one person can dramatically affect the working environment. In some cases, this can be a new leader who is trying to stamp their authority on the organisation, or it can be another worker who may start to undermine the cohesiveness of the team. In both cases, we can observe the impact on the culture, in much the same way as how one rotten apple will eventually turn all the apples in a barrel bad.

Toxicity in the workplace

You may have read about workplace sociopaths and how they create toxicity in the workplace. Most people have seen how narcissism can show up in the upper echelons of any organisation. These types of personalities can be incredibly charismatic and engaging in the beginning, and will only begin to show their true nature after they have engendered a level of dependency or gained control over a person's position in the workplace, and then they will puppeteer and manipulate many and varied situations to maintain their power position. In truth, we can find these types of personalities at all levels in an organisation.

Rather than just maintaining a level of frustration about their presence, I find it a lot easier to understand that personalities that manipulate and try to wield a sense of power and control over others are themselves operating from a false ego position. Underneath this behaviour, you will find a person who has experienced very strong rejection in their early life, combined with extreme levels of criticism from their parents. They are actually full of self-loathing, and they have learned to manipulate and control to make themselves feel better. They often seek the external trappings of success to 'prove' their value and worth to society, whilst inside they feel empty.

The most manipulative approaches in society come from the behaviours identified in narcissistic and borderline personality disorders. When we are trying to understand how people develop, in psychological terms we talk about 'nature vs nurture' — the genetic traits that we are born with vs the characteristics that we develop as a result of our environment. Despite our common understanding that our personality develops from our experiences, these personality disorders have a very strong genetic heritability. The easiest way to describe how these two personalities show up in the world is that their underlying feelings of extreme worthlessness are behind their desire to manipulate and control the behaviour of others to avoid their biggest fear: abandonment.

How we interact with children shapes their sense of self

Personality challenges are far more prevalent in our society than ever before because the changing nature of our society has magnified our childhood experiences of abandonment. Anyone who has engaged in any form of psychological therapy, counselling or self-help reading will have heard about 'issues of attachment'. It's a term almost universally used to explain the difficulties we have in interpersonal relationships — the connections we form with family and friends.

The changing nature of our society has magnified our childhood experiences of abandonment

---

Our changing society post-WWII saw Baby Boomers' growth through the sexual revolution and the adoption of many new social norms. Women increased their participation in the workforce and divorce became more commonplace. The 1980s saw the emergence of centre-based childcare, and Gen Y are the first generation to have experienced this. The bigger impact can be observed in Gen Z, as they were the first generation where almost every child was placed in some form of childcare from an early age.

In Australia, the maternity leave provisions during this time were for 12 months, so most children entered childcare at around 10 months of age. In the United States, some states only allowed six weeks of maternity leave, and mothers in lower socioeconomic groups, including single mothers, were often forced to return to work. This meant that many mothers left their newborn babies in a variety of situations that were not ideal for ensuring that the babies' needs were going to be met. No one recognised the unintended consequences of the impact that this societal expectation would have on our children — the attachment issues that were created by removing the baby's secure attachment figure.

There are a number of reasons why modern parenting may actually be contributing to the increase in mental health issues. It's not about individual parenting techniques, but more about how society and its invalidation of motherhood has actually created bigger issues.

We train our children from birth to not express their needs unnecessarily. Is it any wonder they grow up wondering if they will actually survive? Many of you will understand the notion of using 'controlled crying' techniques with a new baby, the process of leaving a baby who has been fed, bathed, clothed and kept warm to cry themselves to sleep. This aligns with the notion that a child just needs to learn how to 'self-soothe', yet it doesn't align with the baby's survival instincts. Just because we are unable to understand the communication system the baby has (i.e., we don't know 'why' they are crying), we shouldn't decide that their communication is inappropriate and should be ignored. Babies cry out for a connection, and when they don't get it, they experience a disconnect. Trauma. A disturbing event that leaves a wound.

We need connection to survive and when we don't get it it creates a traumatic wound

---

As they grow up, we continue to teach them to dissociate from their own body and their experiences. In the same way that we encourage them to 'self-soothe' by ignoring their crying, we often deny their feelings of pain. When a young child falls over and scrapes their knee, we check to see if there is any blood, and if not, we tell them that they are 'fine'. But they're not fine — they are still in pain. Interestingly, 'magic kisses' work because we are providing the child with validation of the wound, and once we acknowledge the wound, the brain releases numbing chemicals at the surface of the skin making it feel better. These same chemicals are released by rubbing our skin, which is what we naturally do when we bump ourselves. There are normal behavioural training things we do as parents to ensure our children are kept safe, but the way the child stores the belief about themselves in response to this guidance varies greatly depending on their home environment and the parenting style they receive.

Consistency produces security and volatility produces fear and shame

If we compare the generalised health data of countries where children are placed into care from the age of six weeks, we start to see an unwelcome pattern of risk factors for poorer health outcomes. Industrialisation has influenced our effectiveness to raise happy, healthy children, the outcomes of which are starting to become clear.

I can feel the feminists becoming uncomfortable; I really want to make it clear that I am *not* saying women need to be chained to the kitchen and enslaved in domesticity — this isn't the 1950s. However, I think empowered women should be clear that if they choose to have a child, the emphasis being on 'choice', then they probably need to be aware that it is not just an uncomfortable 18 to 24 months of pregnancy and managing the first year.

In reality, a child struggles to cope with big changes in their environment until they are able to more effectively communicate for themselves and start to reason. To do this, they usually require language, so they shouldn't have a lot of caregivers until they are about three years old. Even then, they need to experience smaller chunks of alternative care — not being placed in long day care for ten hours per day from the age of six weeks because mum has to commute an hour each way to an eight-hour work day.

If there is one thing I have learned, it is that when we come across information that makes us angry, it has sparked within us a sense of fear or shame. If what I have just outlined above has upset you, I would encourage you to consider why. If you are a parent who had to put your child into long day care and go to work, it may be a sense of shame that you are feeling at my words. Alternatively, you may not have reached this point in your life yet, but recognise that the only way you can afford to have children is by staying at work. I'm really not suggesting that you are doing the wrong thing here. My point is that as a society we need to value motherhood, and Western societies do not.

The changing nature of society and how children interact with the world has created complex issues that are evident in all areas of our lives. I explore this issue in more depth in my book *The Trouble With Trauma*, which provides further detail about how these experiences impact our lives, and what we can do to resolve this impact.

Suffice to say, it's not hard to see why we have become a stressed, over-worked, over-medicated, egocentric society.

Our work and our self-worth

There are many people who believe they have a great sense of their self-worth, but these people have often built their self-worth on 'what' they do, rather than 'who' they are.

This is extremely common in Western societies and it's growing in Eastern societies. When we recognise that our sense of ourselves is formed through our childhood, when we are encouraged to externalise our feelings and seek validation from external sources about our worth, is it any surprise that many of us think our sense of self is about our work? We have made our 'work' to be our purpose — yet these are entirely unrelated.

If it's not work, we can often validate ourselves through other achievements — sporting or academic achievements. These days we see many young people validate themselves by how many Instagram followers or Facebook friends they have. This is the ultimate externalisation of our perception of ourselves. It's based on what other people, most of whom are complete strangers, think of our image or our experiences.

This is why many young people experience challenges with their mental health, because at the time of their life when they are developmentally programmed to establish connections with their peers, they believe social media platforms represent the reality of those connections.

When Gen X was in high school, we only needed to concern ourselves with the bullies on the school bus, or the rumours going around our year group about us. Although these were traumatic experiences, the bullies could not anonymously attack us, question our actions or tarnish our reputations in a public forum that was theoretically able to be viewed by the whole planet.

Gen Y has engaged in social media for most of their adult life and most have social media accounts for their children from the time that they are born. Gen Z was raised in an age of open access to all sorts of information, thanks to the development of technology. They have no concept of the world before the internet and mobile phones.

Now, I love technology and embrace it, however, I am also aware that when it is not managed well, it can lead to significant problems. I see it a lot when I'm working with children — they have no concept of life without personal devices. Their attention spans are reducing, as is their ability to retain information. After all, they don't need to retain information — they have all the information in the world available at their fingertips.

I'm not a naysayer; I'm a realist. We can't take away the technology, but we can try to raise awareness about balancing its use with other pursuits. The challenge for us as a community, especially in our businesses, is that we need to be able to raise awareness and implement mechanisms that will support our employees to reconnect with themselves. We can do this by validating the healthy expression of emotion in our workplace, rather than just trying to push our perspective over the top of everyone else's. This requires a plan.

Technology is with us to stay, we need to plan downtime away from it

---

Our mental health challenges are the highest in our recorded history. I used to think that it was because we were more mental health literate and we validated the experiences. Although I believe that this is contributing to the increase, I also believe that the combination of changes that have resulted from the industrialisation of our planet has led to the creation of a society that validates learned helplessness.

> **Learned helplessness:** The feeling that a person cannot avoid or control a negative situation, so they stop trying.

How technology is shaping us

Technology enables us to minimise our exposure to discomfort. Our homes and workplaces are heated and cooled to the perfect temperature. We don't need to toil our own garden for food, in fact, we don't even need to cook our food. Many domestic tasks have been reduced by machines that are designed to save time. We've all heard the phrase 'necessity is the mother of invention', but I would have to ask if, in fact, it is 'discomfort' that is the mother of invention.

There are many and varied treatments and recommendations for people to assist them to effectively manage or improve their mental health that are based on forcing yourself into discomfort. It seems the way humans have evolved over time means we have learned to create things that allow us to avoid extremes, thereby staying in a space in which we are not placed under any physiological stress. Although these things have helped us in many ways, it is clear it has been to our detriment.

Discomfort is the driver behind innovative solutions

We no longer have to get uncomfortable about anything, especially in our post-pandemic world. If we actually leave the house to work, we move from air-conditioned houses in air-conditioned cars to air-conditioned offices — many of us don't even do this anymore. We can buy prepared food everywhere, so we don't have to force ourselves to hunt or gather, unless it is at the farmers market on the weekend! We can shop for all our needs online and it gets delivered to our door. If we don't 'feel' like doing anything, we don't have to. We can lie on the couch, watch hours of Netflix and call Uber Eats.

We live our lives on 'autopilot', with no insight into the source of the food we consume or how many chemicals or preservatives we are exposing our gut to, and we take multiple supplements to combat the lack of variety in our diet. Research shows that we produce the majority of our serotonin, our happy hormone, in our gut,[11] so if we don't nourish our bodies, it's no surprise that we don't feel great.

We spend the majority of our waking hours inside, and wear hats, sunglasses and sunscreen when we do venture outside. Yet our brains need light from the sun to function well. Sun exposure activates vitamin D, something that is at chronically low levels in most adults.

We have good community awareness of mental health issues, but often that facilitates dependency rather than supporting recovery. We have created a cycle of dependencies due to the increased pressure we feel to achieve more with less time, without a focus on the true values of our society — connecting with each other.

It is not surprising that we have developed a range of therapeutic interventions that actually help us with our mental health by forcing our bodies into discomfort. From cold water therapies to pushing our physical bodies hard with intensive exercise, we are seeing improvements in mental health through engaging in activities that would have been part of our daily life 'pre-industrialisation'.

We have saved a lot of time from the impact of modernisation to improve the speed and quality of our domestic tasks, however, we haven't taken that time and improved the connection we have with our families. Instead, we have also reduced the time we spend with our children and other members of the family to drive ourselves to improve our financial outcomes, further driving our consumerism. It's a vicious cycle.

Our early experiences shape our future mental health

I hope that you can start to see the pattern emerging: that changes in our world have altered our drive and determination and reduced our resilience. The egocentric modern world has given much more validation to the rights of the individual over the needs of the collective. This is the driver behind the increase in narcissistic and borderline behaviours in the workplace. The genetic predisposition (nature) has been magnified by the changes in our society that have increased attachment problems (nurture), fuelled by a focus on external validation of success rather than building solid beliefs internally about our value.

> **Nature vs nurture:** The genetic traits that we are born with vs the characteristics that we develop as a result of our environment.

This gives rise to self-absorbed behaviour and the active pursuit of validation from others, combined with a sensitivity to rejection and an under-developed emotional self-regulation system. As humans, we need connection to survive. In the absence of a secure connection, we learn to manipulate others to ensure that we can get what we need to survive. If we don't get what we need, we can experience strong emotional reactions that result in an emotional outburst (borderline behaviour) or a controlled, subversive attack (narcissistic behaviour). These behaviours have been learned because they elicit a reliable response, maintaining a connection through the exertion of power (narcissistic) or emotional responsibility (borderline).

Other types of mental health conditions develop in response to traumatic experiences. It's really important to understand that we all experience trauma in our lives due to the nature of our human existence. Most of us understand depression and anxiety as common mental health conditions. In our society, there is often debate about what comes first: depression or anxiety?

Anxiety develops first, and this occurs in childhood. Our first cognitive emotional experience is shame, but the discomfort of shame results in an avoidance of experiencing shame again. Often the first significant experience of shame was quite a surprise to us, something that was completely outside of our control. We become fearful of experiencing it again in the future and we are anxious to avoid it, usually becoming as controlling as we can possibly be of our environment to minimise the fear of the potential shame. Anxiety is really just fear of the future.

Depression develops in adolescence. At this stage in our development, we are trying to differentiate ourselves from our parents and connect with our peers. For the survival of the species, we need to find like-minded peers who accept us. Anxiety is still with us, and we fear the potential rejection by our peers. When we are rejected by our peers, which we all are at some point, we experience shame. We are still learning how to interact with others to obtain a consistent response that enables us to maintain a secure connection to our peers. When we fail, which we all do, we focus our attention on all of the other times that we had similar failures in the past. It's a natural learning process to review our mistakes and try to develop ways to improve our approach and increase our chances of success in the future. However, we can get caught in staying focused on the past and the 'shoulda, coulda, woulda' thoughts that keep us focused on our failure.

Life is a continuous improvement process that requires regular review

---

We need to recognise that we are still growing and learning about the world in our adolescence. We need to recognise our response to rejection, regroup and feel confident to try another approach. This is where the parenting of adolescents often creates more problems.

Parents who have their own unresolved sensitivities to rejection will become over-protective of their teenager and encourage avoidant behaviours. These parents will stand up for their children and take on their battles for them, rather than teaching them how to problem solve different approaches that might achieve success. This is where learned helplessness begins.

This is how the 'passive rejectors' discussed in chapter 1 end up representing 40 per cent of the workers who do nothing in the face of a toxic workplace, because they feel helpless in the face of the seemingly insurmountable problems that develop.

Parents who are self-absorbed, controlling or avoidant will be dismissive of their teenager's feelings, often belittling them, blaming them or ignoring them. These parents will negate the feelings of the teenager in favour of their own emotional experiences (borderline) or they will berate and blame the teenager and tell them to toughen up and be more like them (narcissistic).

Not surprisingly, these become the workers who are often responsible for creating toxic work environments. In order to be validated in any way, they often learn the same emotional manipulation techniques used by their parents, as it is the only way that they can experience any sense of connection. A percentage of them are also represented by the 'active rejectors'. Many who grow up in an environment where their emotional responses were invalidated end up fighting other battles through their adult life.

Parents who take the time to support their teenager to brainstorm options in an attempt to overcome their feelings of rejection, and check in about their success, support healthy decision-making capabilities. These become the 'escapee' workers. The ones who can make a rational assessment around whether or not the workplace culture is likely to change and swiftly act in the face of their assessed evidence.

Case study: Jenny

Jenny experienced a psychological injury in the workplace over a very short period of time. She worked in a community organisation that was dependent on government funding to maintain the service and their employment. A very experienced new coworker was employed, but the level of output wasn't what would have been expected from someone with their expertise. As a result, Jenny and another team member were feeling pressured to take on more work.

The new employee always seemed to have an excuse for why things weren't getting done, and was pressuring others to help. This person would often then pass off other people's work as their own and accept the accolades. Their ability to maintain funding was reliant on the organisation achieving certain key performance indicators (KPIs), which filtered down to each team member who needed to meet individual targets. The new team member would consistently fall short and then put pressure on the rest of the team to help. It became untenable: they were at risk of losing their funding and, thereby, their jobs.

Jenny approached her supervisor with concerns about the disparity in output and questioned the performance management of the new employee. Jenny didn't see any change as a result of this escalation, so she approached the executive officer with another colleague to escalate their concerns. As a result of this escalation, Jenny and her colleague were screamed at by the supervisor. The new employee had become very close with the supervisor and a strong rift developed in the work area.

Jenny started to experience significant levels of anxiety in relation to her workplace. She and her colleague continued to escalate concerns to the executive officer, but nothing was resolved. Jenny's anxieties exacerbated so she escalated the matter further to the founding body and lodged a formal complaint.

An independent investigator was engaged to look at their grievances. They conducted many interviews and Jenny felt that the process wasn't transparent. The new employee made a counter allegation about Jenny and her colleague around placing unreasonable pressure to perform on a new employee.

Jenny reiterated the performance criteria alignment with their KPIs, and the fact they were going to lose their funding if something wasn't done. Despite the fact that she had escalated her concerns and asked for help, nothing was done. In the end, the organisation determined that Jenny and her colleague were harassing the new employee. Jenny immediately went on stress leave and lodged a workers compensation claim, however, the employer decided to dismiss her a month later.

Jenny sought the services of a solicitor and took her case to the Fair Work Commission, who determined that Jenny had been adversely treated in a workplace. However, there was no avenue for her to return to the workplace because of the acrimony.

Despite the fact that Jenny felt vindicated by the outcome, she was left without meaningful employment and that took a significant negative toll on her mental health. Jenny remains out of the workforce almost five years later.

Resolution: Jenny

When we consider Jenny's circumstances, I want to highlight several opportunities for the manager to have taken action that would have enabled a much better outcome for all concerned. Given that the readers of this book are likely to be managers and leaders, I believe that it will be more beneficial to look at the points to turn this around.

Opportunity #1: Hearing Jenny's concerns

When Jenny raised her initial concerns regarding the performance of the colleague, the supervisor had an opportunity to validate the observation, and provide reassurance that the manager had insight into the work performance of the new employee and ownership of the management of them. The manager didn't take the time to unpack all of Jenny's concerns about the performance, and what impact the perception of poor performance was having on Jenny's anxiety.

Action: When a staff member raises concerns with you about the performance of another staff member, take the time to understand the motivation for the escalation. In this case, the supervisor had the opportunity to reassure Jenny that the new employee was on a performance management plan and that the KPIs were being monitored, and remind her that it takes time for any new employee to get up to speed. The supervisor needed to try and understand if Jenny had any other concerns; for example, was there a personality clash between them? Was Jenny's perception about the performance of her new colleague an accurate one? When one staff member has a negative perception of the performance of another, you need to manage that perception. If Jenny's assessment was correct, then it should have been validated. If it was incorrect, then the supervisor needed to take time to understand and help to manage Jenny's perception.

The supervisor should have also taken the time to reassure Jenny that her fears about the impact on their future funding, and therefore the security of their jobs, was something that senior management were very aware of and taking seriously. Then Jenny should have been thanked for raising her concerns, and assured that if they needed any additional input from Jenny, that they would let her know. They should have left the opportunity open for Jenny to raise additional concerns if things didn't appear to be improving over the next month.

Opportunity #2: Supporting your management staff with open dialogue

Next, we note that Jenny escalated her concerns up the line to the executive officer because she felt dismissed by the supervisor, and her anxiety was still not being addressed.

Action: The executive officer seemingly took Jenny's concerns seriously, but they decided to address the ineffective management of the new employee with the supervisor first, putting the supervisor in a position of feeling judged as not effectively managing the new staff member. This placed the supervisor in direct conflict with Jenny because the supervisor felt inadequate after the executive officer intervened. The executive officer should have taken the opportunity to hold a meeting with Jenny and the supervisor to air Jenny's concerns, in the same format as I outlined above for how the supervisor could have handled it.

The executive officer needed to demonstrate to Jenny that her concerns were being taken seriously, and action would be taken to address the perception that appeared to be the source of stress. Trying to facilitate a conciliation between Jenny and the supervisor would eliminate any frustration on the supervisor's behalf about the impact of Jenny's actions on the executive officer's perception of their capability. Not doing this creates the risk that the supervisor will retaliate against Jenny by exerting their power. Finally, the executive officer should have reassured Jenny that the supervisor has their support, but that the door is open if Jenny has any further concerns over the coming month.

Opportunity #3: Transparency and follow through

Jenny responds to her feelings of not being heard by providing ongoing and extensive narratives to the executive officer, in an attempt to achieve some resolution.

Action: If you receive one or multiple emails from your staff member outlining their circumstances, take the time to acknowledge their perspective, even if you don't agree with it. It's still their perspective and deserves to be respected and acknowledged. The executive officer should have acknowledged the concerns and the pain expressed by Jenny, and provided reassurance that the supervisor is handling the performance. However, the executive officer should also assess the accuracy of the supervisor's reporting if they have promised to monitor the issue. There must be a level of transparency, especially if the performance is measurable. If the escalation continues, they must arrange an independent mediation to assess the reality of the concerns raised by Jenny on all affected staff.

Resolution lies in acknowledging the perspective of the person raising concerns, even when you hold a different view

Opportunity #4: Own the problem and the solution

Due to the ongoing inactivity and the division in the work area, Jenny escalates her concerns to yet another higher authority. It is highly unlikely, at this stage, that there is no validity to Jenny's concerns. In reality, the inaction has created a much bigger problem and now turned the workplace toxic. The team is divided, and productivity has reduced even further because Jenny is searching for further evidence to support her claim, in addition to evidence of the inaction of the management team. The introduction of an investigator makes all employees feel like they are being accused of something. Jenny is now ostracised as the troublemaker by two levels of management, both of whom will be negating their own ineffective management of Jenny's concerns by trying to scapegoat her.

Action: Management should have communicated openly with all areas of the organisation that Jenny has raised some serious concerns, and that an independent investigation is being undertaken as a matter of urgency. They should have asked that all employees who are not directly affected not involve themselves with the process, as it is important to afford the investigator a clear picture of the challenges.

It's important for the executive officer to set expectations for the transparency of the findings, if appropriate, but reassure teams there will be action regardless. They should have communicated that 'work will continue', but that it is important to clarify these concerns, expressed gratitude for Jenny's commitment and disappointment that it had to get to this point. Reiterating that the focus of leadership is on maintaining funding for the service and guaranteeing job security for all employees would have reassured employees of their priorities. When situations like these occur, reinforce your ownership of the problem in allowing it to get to this point, and the need to focus on ongoing important work.

Opportunity #5: Supporting the employee with compassion

The investigation was met with a counter-claim and, in the final report, produced an adverse finding against Jenny and her colleague. Careful consideration needs to be given to the implications of making the findings public, in this case, sharing the outcome information with other staff.

Action: Clear communication that the process is complete and the findings are being addressed needs to be provided to all staff. Acknowledgement of the failings in the management process should be shared, as well as the steps that will be taken to ensure that this type of situation won't arise again. The executive officer should have arranged a private meeting on a Monday morning with the adversely impacted staff member to discuss the investigators report, offering them the opportunity to have a support person with them.

Don't *ever* arrange these meetings last thing on a Friday afternoon — it's a sign of your discomfort and desire to avoid the conflict

---

It's a sure-fire way to make sure the adversely impacted staff member will not return to the workplace.

Open the conversation by acknowledging your own failure as leader in this situation. Communicate the adverse findings coupled with a sincere desire to resolve things, and provide the staff member with support to ensure that this doesn't happen again. Reinforce the value of the staff member to the organisation and the team, and offer mediation to broker an improved working environment for all team members. Provide the affected team member with some external coaching support, starting immediately after the meeting. Ask the affected team member to keep the outcomes confidential, as the thing that is important to the cohesiveness of the team is that a resolution has been achieved.

Ask the staff member if there is anything that they need to help them to 'recover at work' as this might be quite a shock. Try to discourage a significant period of leave as we know that it increases distress and promotes avoidant behaviour. Make time to check in each day with the staff member, ask how they are travelling and if there is anything that they need help with.

Trauma: What is it?

Trauma is at the base of what psychologists refer to as psychopathology: the negative psychological problems we experience that cause us difficulties in life; the feelings and experiences we refer to as mental illness.

It's important to be clear about what I mean by 'trauma', because many people, especially in Western cultures, believe that traumatic events are only things that are life threatening, involving some physical threat. They think of events that are hugely impactful: rape, accidents, natural disasters. It is true, these events are absolutely traumatic, but so are the things that threaten our ability to connect. This is because, to your brain, they are *viewed as the same*.

The word 'trauma' comes from the Greek word for 'wound'. It means a deeply distressing or disturbing experience. Over time, it has grown to mean more, especially in psychological circles; however, I really want to come back to the original meaning because I believe that the way modern psychology has viewed trauma isn't helpful for understanding what it really is and how it impacts our development. My perspective is based on the original Greek meaning: it is an event that creates a wound, an emotional wound that develops from a distressing or disturbing experience. To our brain, a disconnection is a distressing experience.

Trauma is an emotional wound that creates a disconnect, a distressing experience

---

It is important to ensure clarity on this point because when we consider the modern psychological interpretation of trauma, we have taken it to imply that an inability to cope with a traumatic experience is a failing on the part of the human who experiences it. Yet, the way our brain approaches traumatic experience is entirely normal — and, arguably, it is also completely developmentally appropriate!

We *all* experience trauma. Yet, we are told as a society that we shouldn't focus on it. Our inability to 'not' focus on it, or to repress the impact of the trauma, is considered by the fathers of modern psychology as some sort of neurosis.

It isn't.

It is the failure to recognise the 'normality' of traumatic experience that has put us where we are now as a society: over-worked, over-medicated, avoidant and judgemental.

Why we need to understand the impact of trauma

We need to change this approach if we want to improve our lives, and the lives of generations to come.

It is the failure to recognise trauma as a normal experience that requires review and routine processing, that is responsible for the majority of our mental health issues today.

I firmly believe that if we understood trauma and its impact, and we were taught the processes to resolve it, we could eliminate the most common mental health issues from our society in a few generations

---

How trauma results in mental health problems

It is essential that leaders understand traumatic experiences, and why we should minimise the traumatic impact of your workplace on your people. Our ability to function as effective human beings depends on how we process our traumatic experiences. Our very first experience of a traumatic event, the first that we make an attribution and blame ourselves for, usually happens when we are about four years old. Our first experience of trauma is realistically earlier in our life, but the first abandonment that we experience *and take responsibility for* occurs before we start primary school.

Why does this happen to us at the age of four? Well, as human beings we have a really interesting developmental experience from the time we are born.

Children express their needs from an early age

When we are born, our emotional and physical needs are met by our primary caregivers: our mother/father or other adults who looked after us as a baby. Our needs are usually always met; we are fed, clothed and have a roof over our head. Hopefully, when we cry to indicate that we have a need, we have a secure bond to a caregiver who will meet that need. In this way we can feel reasonably secure and can grow and feel nurtured.

Around 18 months old, things change quite significantly. Toddlers start to learn language and express themselves — they start to say 'no!' They are exploring language and noticing what gets a reaction. Children view these interactions as important, and they notice the reaction they get when they say 'no!' They will often repeat behaviours as their brain is learning from these reactions and coding their memory with positive and negative experiences. However, at this age, toddlers do not have a direct or clear understanding about what it all means — their brain is trying to learn how the world works and they test certain behaviours to see the reaction. Do they get what they want or not? This will determine whether or not they should repeat a behaviour.

Expressing desires is more complex

Around the age of two children develop 'desire' — which is very different to 'need'. So, what's the big issue about how desire moulds us?

At this stage, children change their focus from what is given to them to meet their needs, and suddenly have a *desire* for something different. The problem is that children don't understand why, up until now their caregivers have given them what they *needed*, but don't appear to do the same with what they *want*. The toddler gets frustrated because they think the primary caregivers know exactly what they're thinking, because until that point, the caregiver intuitively 'knew' what they needed — toddlers are very egocentric.

But when 'need' changes to 'desire', they look to the parent to give them what they want and they don't necessarily get it!

This is why toddlers throw tantrums. They don't have the language to communicate their desires, and if they're not getting what they want, they will throw a tantrum in frustration. The responses at this age are actually developmentally appropriate. It isn't 'wrong' or 'bad' — it's *normal* for to have this frustration response at this age. Developmentally, children have two main emotions at this stage — sadness and frustration — and they often swing from one to the other very quickly.

From this point toddlers develop more language, and become more aware, but they still believe the parent can understand what's going on in their head. In fact, they believe that all the adults around them can read their minds.

Individuation takes longer to develop

There is that moment when we know that children develop true and full individuation. Young children — toddlers — will usually be able to look in the mirror and say their name. I can point in the mirror and say 'Kerry' (in my case). I know that's the name we give that baby or that person I see in the mirror. However, we don't actually realise that the baby is *me*, that I am an individual, because at that point I still see myself as an extension of my parent... Until the age of four.

Around four years of age, children work out that they can know things, or that little voice inside their head knows things their parents don't know unless they tell them. When a child reaches that point of true individuation, that is the point when they know they are an individual and that what they think 'inside my head', their caregiver cannot know unless they express it. A four-year-old will come to you and say, 'I've got a secret!' This is when we become truly an individual.

With individuation comes responsibility

What I find quite amusing is that soon after developing individuation, we learn to tell lies.

Why is this important? Because from that point, we understand that the things that happen to us happen because we impact them. What we know about children up until around the age of ten is they have what we refer to as 'concrete thinking'. Good things happen to us because we're good, and bad things because we're bad. Simple as that, black and white.

If you reflect on your early childhood, you may be aware of when individuation happened for you, that moment around the age of four. You will have had a moment, after you recognised you were an individual, when you felt an abandonment or a disconnection from your primary caregivers. At this point, you rationalised to yourself that it was your fault.

The awareness of the impact of this moment is critically important, because this is the child part that, later on, you tap back into when you are feeling rejected — your first experience of an abandonment. In fact, it is this part of yourself that forms the true basis of your personality or ego — the root of who you truly are as an individual. Our 'inner child', the four-year-old.

Shame and fear come from abandonment

When we experience abandonment, we feel a lot of 'shame'. Recall that, at this time in our life, we feel we are fully responsible for the things we experience — so we spend our time trying to ensure we don't have this experience again. We are trying to avoid potential rejection in the future.

As children, when we experience that sense of abandonment, our primary emotional response is shame. We don't like this feeling, so we seek to avoid being rejected in the future, hopefully alleviating the experience of shame. As such, we start to become fearful about being rejected and we develop a level of anxiety, because anxiety is based in fear.

These are our two heaviest and most basic negative emotions: shame and fear. Shame is focused on the past, and later becomes the basis for potential depression. Fear, in contrast, is future focused and is the basis of anxiety.

This is a key understanding for humanity to recognise — all children experience anxiety, as fear is the most common emotion in our early childhood. So, most children of primary-school age experience anxiety. How they cope with managing their anxiety is directly dependent on their home environment, as the focus of security in our early life is directed towards our family connection.

In contrast, depression doesn't actually develop until later, in our adolescence. Interestingly, it's the primary driver of adolescence to work out who you in are comparison to your parents and family. In adolescence, we turn to our peers to obtain connection — we want to be like our friends, not our family. We are trying desperately to work out who we are as individuals in comparison to our friends. The inability to obtain a secure connection with our peers leads to increased anxiety and, ultimately, depression. This is why the rates of depression in young people are recorded at around 50 per cent — but I would argue that *all* human beings experience low mood during their adolescence, we just don't all talk about it!

Vulnerability can lead to new connections

When we understand the impact of shame, and are aware of the paralysing impacts of fear, we can understand why Brené Brown talks so passionately about vulnerability. You see, our human experiences of shame and fear result in a disconnection that can be moderated by the expression of vulnerability. When we are prepared to be courageous and share our experiences of shame with others, this affords us an opportunity to also form a new connection with another human being because we connect over our shared experiences.

The challenge for us as human beings is that our childhood experiences impact our capacity to be courageous. These childhood experiences have a psychological impact and change the wiring of our brains due to our human capacity for neuroplasticity — but these changes also impact our biology, our cellular functioning and our immune system.

I deal more with these concepts and how our traumatic experiences impact our growth as individual human beings in my book, *The Trouble With Trauma*.

The impact of trauma

It's essential that we understand the impact of trauma on our health, because it is not just the psychological distress that causes problems; there are also multiple physical problems that can develop as a result of our traumatic experiences.

When a traumatic event occurs, we naturally seek to identify a reason for it. This attribution is where the challenge begins, because if a person takes responsibility for the traumatic event, either due to their actions or lack of action, then the event will develop into a traumatic injury.

Traumatic injuries can create much bigger problems for an individual in terms of their behaviour and their other stress responses, like sleep, mood and appetite. Traumatic events induce high levels of stress in the body, releasing cortisol and increasing heart rate and generally raising the level of inflammation in the body. You may have heard the term 'stress response' in reference to how our physical body and our psychological processes are intertwined.

Stress response: Sometimes referred to as 'fight or flight', it is a combination of physical and psychological reactions to a stress event.

It is common for physical injuries to cause psychological problems and vice versa. We don't need to look very hard to find evidence of how our physical body responds to the stress of modern-day life. In fact, these days we can find evidence of our physiological responses quite easily just by looking at the data collected by your smart watch.

Neurological research has come a long way in the past ten to 15 years. As technology improves, we see much more research being published about the impact traumatic events have on our body and our brain. There is more and more evidence showing the negative consequences of long-term exposure to high levels of cortisol (from heart disease to stroke), as cortisol creates inflammation in the body.[12]

More than this, the long-term impacts of high levels of stress on our mental health and wellbeing are now really clear. The pandemic has provided a fantastic example of how long-term hyperarousal, caused by a prolonged activation of our natural fear response, can erode our mental health state over time. There are significant reasons why we should seek to reduce stress in our lives and resolve the impact of traumatic events as quickly as possible.

Depending on your family circumstances growing up, your 'trauma baggage' may be small or significant. Even if you grew up in a very supportive and comfortable household, you will carry with you a sense of not being good enough in some area of your life, even if you spend a lot of time trying not to focus on it. This is because of how we develop over the course of our lives. We all have traumatic experiences and we all experience triggering events — sometimes we are triggered by events in the workplace.

Trauma in the workplace

Traumatic experiences in the workplace can occur for many reasons, but we have some pretty clear ideas about the issues that cause the biggest negative psychological impacts.

In general terms, the workplace hazards that create risks of harm to mental health are known as psychosocial hazards. These hazards can cause both psychological and physical harm.

> **Psychosocial hazards:** Aspects of the workplace that have the potential to cause a person physical or psychological harm.

Psychosocial hazards can be created by the way the work or job is designed, organised and managed. This may include the equipment, working environment or requirements to undertake duties in hazardous environments (occupational risks). They are also created through working relationships and interactions, including discrimination, bullying, harassment, aggression and violence.

Our most common psychosocial hazards cluster around several factors that are linked to invalidation or a lack of personal control. These hazards all create traumatic experiences for the individual due to how these experiences are perceived. When we think of these psychosocial hazards, we can see a clear delineation in what kinds of behaviours trigger them:

- invalidation: negative impacts from harassment and bullying, lack of recognition, ineffective organisational justice, isolated workers and poor support

- lack of personal control: negative impacts around job control, role clarity, job demands, workplace interactions and physical environment, including remote work.

When we want to understand why these traumatic experiences expose the worker to a psychosocial risk, we need to understand the mediating effect of how the individual perceives the approach. In essence, when categorising our negative experiences, we take two main emotional pathways (which should, by now, sound familiar): shame or fear. At its most basic level, it is then easy to see how many potentially negative interactions can create an expression of fear or shame in the workplace. The extent of the impact is mediated by a whole lot of interpersonal variables based on culture, self-worth, authority and confidence. Regardless of the extent, the impact is still traumatic.

Why tackle trauma in the workplace?

In my book *The Trouble With Trauma*, I outline how the ability to connect with others and share similar experiences can assist us to feel more positive or negative about ourselves, as we use these similarities to validate our own feelings and life experiences. As human beings, we are always looking to our 'outer world' (our immediate environment) to help explain our 'inner world', the thoughts, feelings and behaviours we feel responsible for.

Any disagreement with another human being raises the potential for rejection. When you experience any form of conflict as an adult, you are drawing on the combined emotional experiences of your whole life in how you respond. Our primary emotional need as a human being is for connection; how we react in any disagreement is going to be influenced by our childhood and parental relationships, and then this is mediated by how many times we have experienced rejection over the course of our lives. We are all sensitive to rejection, we have just learned to manage our responses to the potential for it in different ways.

What does that have to do with work? You may ask. An awful lot more that we think!

As I have outlined, the notion that we can have a clear separation between life and work is a fallacy. It's an ideological perspective promoted by capitalism to try to reduce distractions in the work environment. Thankfully, the pandemic has done a lot to elevate awareness of psychological distress in our community — so much so that we have many people who are more aware that they may need help or benefit from therapeutic support. Prior to the pandemic, one in five people reported a mental health issue, now it's four in five people who report psychological distress.

As with many areas of human knowledge, growth and awareness, we can see widespread change in our attitudes in a short period of time. Over the past three years we have developed greater mental health literacy; however, we still hold unrealistic expectations that our governments are going to provide a solution to the problem. We talk about needing greater access to professional services, yet our mental health professionals can't possibly meet the demand, and many have felt so completely overwhelmed by the pressure placed upon them that they have chosen to retire all together.

We have to help ourselves!

Or in the case of a workplace, we have to try not to create the traumatic experiences in the first place. We can't ignore behaviour and think that if a person needs help, they will sort it out later. Besides — prevention is always a hundred times better than cure!

Employee assistance programs

Most corporate entities will offer their staff the opportunity to access some sort of Employee Assistance Program (EAP) or other early intervention support for staff who identify that they are having some challenges. Access to such support programs does vary across businesses in the Western world. Whether staff are supported through their medical benefits or some other service provision, many have access to psychological support for their challenges, regardless of whether these issues are caused by the work environment or other life experiences.

The reality is that most modern psychological approaches don't afford the opportunity to fully resolve our traumatic experiences. In many ways, modern therapy teaches us to try and tolerate the impact of our emotional experiences. It has not been an unreasonable approach to take, given that we didn't have any other way to manage except to try and learn to 'cope' with the feelings. However, our understanding of many things in science has come a very long way, and I don't think that modern medicine, or therapeutic approaches, have moved as quickly.

There are many reasons for this — arguably, psychological ones! It is the tendency to be firm in our 'beliefs' that usually creates bigger problems. In essence, as human beings, we tend to hold tight to a particular way of viewing the world when we have had experiences that affirm the effectiveness of a particular approach.

This is actually representative of a common psychological phenomenon known as a *confirmation bias*. This is based on the notion that when we have to strongly defend a position that we have taken on an issue, we often fight harder for that position, and hold much tighter to it, than if we had been more open to an alternative perspective in the first place.

> **Confirmation bias:** When the act of defending a belief strengthens the individual's commitment to that belief.

There are many reasons why we form cognitive biases. They do support our system to make rational and effective decisions quickly. Think of them like little shortcuts that your brain has set up in a complex system that allows you to quickly categorise experiences — but sometimes we get it wrong.

Interestingly, if we realise that we 'got it wrong', we have applied an *attribution bias,* which results in *cognitive dissonance,* a psychological phenomenon in which we hold two or more opposing beliefs, values or ideas about something. Our brain doesn't like conflicting information and it causes us quite a lot of psychological discomfort. So, in order to resolve the discomfort, we almost over-subscribe to the new way of thinking. To be able to change our first opinion, we must become a champion of the new cause.

As a result, you will find that, when you have developed strong beliefs about a particular issue, you will hold tighter to those beliefs if they are ever 'challenged'. If you have felt the need to defend those beliefs at any point, then your commitment to that belief becomes stronger. This is the basis for all of the extremism in the world and it manifests in many areas of our society, between cultures, in mainstream religions and in the workplace.

Cognitive dissonance: The discomfort an individual experiences when they hold two conflicting beliefs, values or ideas.

You can start to understand why we need to prevent the challenges arising as much as we possibly can, rather than trying to patch things up after the issue has developed. As I am sure you can appreciate, sometimes our concrete ways of thinking as human beings, are not conducive to developing innovative solutions to complex issues. If you want to ensure a different outcome you *must* approach the same situation differently.

If you want to heal a workplace, you must change attitudes, ensure consistency and show up each and every day with respect and compassion for your people.

Part II
The Role of Leadership

CHAPTER 3

Compassionate Leadership

The key to psychological safety at work

When a new organisation is referred to me, it is often because the leader is new to the workplace and they are experiencing difficulties with the culture. I am regularly called into environments where the toxicity of the culture is extreme. I am constantly amazed at how some businesses continue to function, let alone remain profitable. Alternatively, the leader may have become aware of the magnitude of an emerging problem, for example, if the rate of psychological injury claims has recently escalated. At other times, they reach out because they're aware of a high rate of absenteeism in a particular section, or the profitability of one area of the business has dropped significantly.

In business, we don't spend enough time focused on the prevention of these issues. We wait until it has developed into a really big problem, and then we look to an external consultant to come in and fix it. Although developing a strategy to repair a toxic culture requires a unique skill set, finding the right person to support you as a leader to unpack the complexity of how the situation developed is challenging. Often the leader is embarrassed by the situation because they feel responsible for it, even in cases where they might be new to the role. The more compassionate a leader is, the more they feel some inadequacy in not being able to resolve the problem for themselves.

Get to know your people

Often when a leader is new to a role, especially if they were recruited to 'fix' the business, they will come into an organisation and immediately start asking questions to ascertain the problems. Depending on your people, this will immediately result in them closing ranks, and the new leader can find themselves extremely frustrated that they are not able to access the information that they need to make decisions.

What if I told you that the best thing a new leader, a compassionate leader, can do in a new role is spend time with their team, asking them about the business and their role in it? If you have been handed a mandate by a board or other hierarchy, you need to meet with *all* staff in an organisation-wide meeting in the first week that you are on the job. Introduce yourself, your background and experience, your mandate and the rationale for it, as well as reiterating to staff your vision for the business and how that aligns with the current mission of the organisation. In this way, you establish the groundwork for what the future will look like and why you, as the new leader, are the right person to get the business there — but acknowledging that you absolutely can't deliver this vision without their support. You then need to let them know that you will be meeting with each and every one of them over the coming weeks (depending on the size of the organisation) and you want to hear three things from them: the thing they love about working here, their biggest frustration in working here, and the one thing they would like you to change in the business.

The best thing a compassionate new leader can do is spend time with their team seeking their perspectives on the business

---

The reason that I recommend this approach to every new leader is because it engenders a sense of clarity about who you are and what you are there to do. It also affords your people an opportunity to get a measure of you, what your values are and your vision for their future. By demonstrating a sense of inclusivity by asking for their feedback, you provide all employees with a feeling that they have a voice. When you follow this up with a personal interaction, no matter how brief, they feel that they are important to you.

Dealing with confidentiality: how much should you tell them?

Many leaders who are brought in to fix a problem are often told not to let the staff know about the problem. I see this a lot in large corporates, where the CEO is appointed by a board, and the board will often direct the new CEO to say nothing to the staff because the challenges that the business is facing happened on the board members' watch and they are embarrassed by it. This is the approach taken in most US-based corporates because of sensitivities around the business being sued by the outgoing leadership if there is any insinuation that their leadership was responsible for the difficulties the business now finds itself in. As a leader, I would encourage you to find a way to communicate the 'reality' of the business situation without pointing any fingers.

If the reality check is not communicated to your people, they will not understand the approach that you take to get a measure of the position of the business, and they will resist. There is nothing better to embed a sense of teamwork than working together to find a solution to a problem.

Inclusive leadership

A good leader, an inclusive leader, will bring their team into their inner circle and utilise the challenges to engender trust. Many leaders, however, believe that they were recruited because they have the skill set to sort out the business problem and they already know the solution to the problem — that's why they were hired as the leader!

I recognise that you do have the necessary skills and experience to sort it out for yourself. You could dictate the solution to the problem, and the team is going to do as you tell them. However, this approach is guaranteed to elongate the process and create a lot of staffing problems along the way. Such leadership methods tend to result in high levels of staff turnover and a significant drop in productivity for the first six to 12 months.

When this approach is taken in a toxic workplace, the new leader has the finger pointed at them as the problem because those who were contributing to the creation of the toxicity see that they might be under scrutiny. They will often close ranks against the new leader. As leader, you need to ensure that the board understands that things are going to be challenging for the first 12 months, and that you have their unwavering support to enact change. I have seen many leaders left out on their own by a board that didn't want to accept responsibility for their failings with the previous leadership, and when faced with the revolt of toxic staff, the new leader becomes an easy scapegoat.

Eliminating silos with transparency

Significant leadership turnover can be a by-product of new senior leadership, but it doesn't have to be. Toxic cultures thrive on miscommunication, so a compassionate leader needs to take the helm by communicating consistently with *all* staff and not allowing any other leaders in the business to control the story. Boards need to understand that change can create significant disruption in the business, and avoid jumping to conclusions and assuming that high staff turnover following a change of leadership is indicative of a problem with the leader. It's usually a misconception around what the leader is trying to achieve, and a regular, single point of communication about the change process is the best approach to maintain stability.

Toxicity is perpetuated by silos in large organisations, enabling different areas of the organisation to be closed off to other sections, which can change the messaging significantly. The larger an organisation grows, the more challenging it is to make sure that there is a consistency of approach, especially in communication. The culture of an organisation is always led from the top. If there is a perception that you are not being inclusive or not providing opportunities to engage with people and ask for feedback and input, then it will just create more toxicity down the line. The leader sets the culture. A closed leader is the one who operates in a 'command and control' way, which only works in military environments. It doesn't work effectively in corporate environments, where people expect openness and collaboration, and want to be engaged in supporting the business to succeed.

The leader sets the culture from the top but must be open and inclusive to reduce toxicity

---

Understanding the culture

The leadership approach may need to change based on the industry or the nature of the work. It's essential for a new leader to understand what the culture has been previously, because if you are going to try and change it, you need to do it incrementally, with a lot of engagement and buy-in. Under no circumstances should you go into an organisation that has a toxic culture and attempt to stamp your authority on it. As a new leader, you need to spend the first three months just getting to know your people and the problems that they are having in the business before you start discussing any type of change program.

Being a compassionate leader is really the awareness that your role is not just about how you manage a person and their work deliverables.

It's about understanding that they are a person, and they bring all their challenges in their life, their reality, their external world and their home life to their work environment. When they show up in your workplace, a compassionate leader actually takes into account what is going on for that person each day of their life, and is flexible enough to makes adjustments as needed. Truly compassionate leaders encourage their people to really want to show up and focus for the time that they have available, because they feel valued.

The leadership lottery

In my interview with Stuart Bartels, executive director of the Australian Institute of Police Management (AIPM), he referred to research from the Western Australia Police which identified that member's perceived their outcomes in psychological safety were dependent on the 'leadership lottery' (more on this in chapter 7).

> **Leadership Lottery:** The perception that the outcome of challenging situations in the workplace is directly dependent on the mental health literacy and people management flexibility of the line manager in providing support.

It is this reality that formed the basis for me writing this book. Unfortunately, the majority of corporate environments around the world tend to promote staff to managerial positions without actually undertaking any assessment of their leadership capability. Many people are surprised to learn that leadership is a group of attributes, not a skill, therefore it is innate to an individual, not something that they can learn on a course. Leadership theories abound, but are agreed to be defined by the Big Five model of personality structure.[13]

An attribute is defined as 'a quality or feature regarded as a characteristic or inherent part of someone or something'. Whereas a skill can be considered 'the ability to do something well; expertise' or to 'train (a worker) to do a particular task'. When we consider that leadership is an attribute, you may demonstrate good leadership skill, but you can't be easily trained to be a good leader. You can train to be a great manager, because management capability is a skill not an attribute.

We need checks and balances

One of the challenges in the modern workplace is that the line supervisor has been set up to be the single decision-maker over access to entitlements and support in the workplace. Depending on the size of the organisation, there may be a HR manager or perhaps even a whole area dedicated to HR management, but the majority of businesses in most Western countries tend to minimise their investment in HR management.

The recommended ratio for HR-trained personnel to workers is 1:8, whereas most Westernised corporates operate on a 1:25 ratio. The role of HR is completely undervalued in a world driven by profits, as the HR personnel are considered to be the 'soft' managers, non-revenue-generating resources that take away from the bottom line of the company profits.

It is important that corporate entities start to see the true value of HR managers, not just as the 'payroll' people, but for their expertise as the empathetic leaders of your people. They should also fill the role of quality control manager around people decisions. Most larger businesses have HR policies and procedures, but it is rare that these are regularly reviewed, and even less likely that they are audited for compliance. As such, a line manager may make a decision that is different to the intent of a policy or contrary to procedure, yet most organisations have no escalation pathway to review the decision of a line manager.

Yet, what many corporates fail to realise is that the HR managers enable the workers to operate efficiently and effectively. The ability to feel supported by your employer to manage the day-to-day challenges of life and contribute as much as possible around them is positively correlated to greater productivity.[14] The outcomes of COVID-19 research on productivity in those industries that were able to keep delivering a service during the initial lockdowns are testament to this phenomenon.

When an individual believes that they are valued and supported, they are far more inclined to work to their full capacity. We rely on feeling valued, not always on feeling recognised. As such, when the pandemic stopped many businesses from trading, many employees felt so grateful that they still had a job that they became even more productive.

There are many reasons for this — humans are very complex beings and different societies value work, and support for family life, differently. However, the basic need to be able to earn a living and support your family is still at the core of the desire for employment — then we overlay other social contexts, like status and recognition. Being supported during a time that affected every human being on the planet had a significant impact on workers.

Productivity is not driven by recognition, rather it is a product of feeling valued

---

What makes our people happy?

As human beings, we strive for happiness, yet most people find happiness difficult to define. The definition for one person is going to be completely different to the definition proposed by another. Sadly, I often hear people talk about happiness as an ideal that can't be achieved. Yet, for most people, the idealised view of happiness is that it is a destination, not a constant state. The pursuit of happiness is something that human beings have focused on for millennia, seemingly without real success. Perhaps we just need to adjust our perspective.

There are many leaders who would argue that it's not their job to keep their people happy. However, if you don't keep your people happy in the workplace, they will usually find a workplace that will.

There are common attributes of workplaces in which people report that they are happy at work.[15] If we look at the indicators of healthy and happy work environments, we can start to see patterns such as autonomy over their work output, being valued and well remunerated, and having a good work-life balance. It's the sense of being valued, and how we perceive that we are valued can vary greatly between individuals. I believe the key here is to understand the personalities of your people and ensure that you have regular opportunities to communicate and check in, not just about the progress of work but how your people are tracking with life in general.

When I work with an organisation, one of the first things I seek to understand is the personality distribution of the teams. Depending on the size of the organisation, this can be quite a complex task; however, we usually see that teams tend to cluster in personality traits around the leader. This is often why we can develop issues within a particular section of an organisation.

Despite the variability in these assessments and the numerous criticisms of personality assessments, it can be helpful to have a framework that allows us to broadly group people together. Humans naturally like to categorise things we interact with regularly; it helps us to make an assessment of our environment, even if this may not be the most accurate assessment.

Most large corporates will undertake some form of personality profiling or assessment prior to a person being offered a position. In some industries, this is something that happens routinely, whereas others never consider it. This type of recruitment process also follows trends and, over time, we see new 'profiling' processes that are sold to corporates as the next big thing! Yet, all modern personality profiling is based on the original work of psychologist Carl Jung.

Categorising our attributes

Carl Jung is considered one of the 'fathers' of psychology, along with Sigmund Freud and William James. In his first published work[16] around personality types, published in 1913, Jung theorised that humans cluster around several elements that he broke down into eight parts.

Jung's theory began with the premise that our human consciousness is a self-regulating structure present at birth, so our awareness of our world is just a reality of life. He believed that our awareness is centred in an individual person (ego) who expresses two different attitudes (introversion or extroversion) through four functions in an effort to balance our emotional regulation (psyche).[16]

He described the four functions as two pairs of opposites — thinking and feeling, intuition and sensation — with an individual's dominant mode of functioning being somewhere on each continuum of opposites. In this way it forms a cross, and an individual's functions can be plotted and compared to others' in a way that is balanced and clear and without judgement. Fiona Ross, writing for the Society of Analytical Psychology, summed it up in this way:

Consciousness was seen by Jung as a product of both rational and irrational processes of encountering and assessing reality. Sensation and Intuition are the irrational functions in the sense of their being perceptive, data gathering modes. Thinking (objective) and Feeling (subjective) are the rational functions: they are ways of processing information and making decisions. Sensation tells us that a thing is, Thinking tells us what the thing is and Feeling tells us what it is worth to us. Intuition is about trusting hunches.[16]

Jung's work was groundbreaking because it created a system to help us understand the most complicated of beings — ourselves — and compare the results to others'. It was very different to other systems that were far more focused on the neuroses, or judgements, about what was wrong or different with a person.

The Myers-Briggs Type Inventory (MBTI) was devised by a pioneering mother and daughter in order to put Jungian typology to practical use outside of psychological circles. They built on Jung's work with the addition of perception and judgement, to create 16 different types, each type identifying the dynamic relationship between attitude and functions for any individual.[16]

Many people have built teams based on the MBTI, despite the fact that the foundational principles of the work have been criticised for an apparent lack of applied academic rigour in its development, something that wasn't available to two women in the 1940s. The MBTI as an assessment tool definitely found its place in the corporate world post-WWII, and fuelled the growth of individuation in the workplace. The application into the corporate world really spread the knowledge of Jungian typology and gave validation to personality differences and how they show up in the workplace.

Personality testing affords us some insight into the way individuals tend to operate in daily life, but they are not the be-all and end-all cure for ensuring a balanced corporate culture. What they do enable us to see is whether or not we have balance in our business.

Quadrants

When we undertake a personality test based on Jung's types, what we are provided with is a categorisation of our preferred traits, and this should give us a reasonably good picture of how a person will behave 90 per cent of the time. I find it easier to draw it for people using a quadrant model and then plot everyone onto one chart (see figure 3.1, overleaf). This can be done for a team or for a whole organisation, depending on the problem that we are trying to solve.

	DATA		
R E F L E C T I O N	**Information Processing** *Detail orientated* *Planner* *Bottom-up* **Sensing (S)**	**Structure** *Results Focussed* *Orderly* *Established* **Judging (J)**	**Decision Making** *High Expectations* *Analytical* *Independent* **Thinking (T)**	A C T I O N
	Focus *Internal* *Subjective* *Introspective* **Introverted (I)**	C → ■ ← D S → ← I	**Focus** *External* *Objective* *Assertive* **Extroverted (E)**	
	Decision Making *Gut Feeling* *Harmonious* *People Oriented* **Feeling (F)**	**Structure** *Spontaneous* *Flexible* *Adaptive* **Perceiving (P)**	**Information Processing** *Big Picture* *Strategic* *Top-down* **Intuitive (I)**	
	PEOPLE		

Figure 3.1: Quadrant model. How I outline the different elements for organisations before I map each staff member into the quadrant model to identify personality clustering. A useful process to assist in identifying gaps in personality types to support recruitment for diversity. This model was inspired the MBTI and DISC models, and my own interpretation of Jungian types.

Understanding where the personality types cluster, and where the outliers are, is very important in trying to understand why there may be a problem in an organisation. In most cases, the 'problem' can be defined by the outliers, as humans will naturally group with like-minded others. Group dynamics will then kick in to further separate the 'us' and 'them', resulting in the group lacking cohesion.

When I am asked to consult for an organisation that has high staff turnover and low productivity, we often see little or no clustering.

In reality, every business needs to be able to cover all of the attitudes, functions and constructs of decision-making to be effective. In order to be successful, each business unit requires a balance of personality types to ensure that things move forward based on an effective assessment of all the possibilities applicable to the work. When the team is balanced, you are assured that the future focus of the business area is balanced, and everyone is moving in the same direction. However, in order to achieve this balance, and thereby success, we need to actively build balanced teams and educate them about why they need differing perspectives. We have to train them to value their opposite, rather than seek to separate themselves from them.

When you recruit into an organisation, you need a good spread of personality types. When you understand what your personality types are, it's easier to create some buy-in, because you can appeal to the different elements of what each person's personality is going to need to function effectively.

Working with different personality types

If you find that there are difficulties between people in the workplace, we can often tie this to the differing personality types, and how they approach the work. If you have a senior leader who is a big-picture, strategic thinker, and a colleague who is very detail oriented, their working relationship can be frustrating as there is resistance at both ends. The creative-thinking leader will be frustrated because they have a vison, and they communicate it to the colleague who they expect to support them in creating a plan to bring the vision to life. They will often experience a significant communication mismatch because the detail-oriented person doesn't have the information they need, and they can't connect the vision to their current work. So we have to make that link.

Finding the needle in the haystack

One of the best analogies I use to explain this disconnect is to imagine how these two different personality types would approach a needle in a haystack. The big-picture strategic mindset asks the detail-oriented person for help with the task. The dialogue looks something like this:

Leader pops his head into George's office: *Oh, George, I really need your help for this very important task. Can you please help me find the needle in the haystack? That'd be great. I have to go. I have an important meeting, but I look forward to seeing the needle when you find it. I'll catch you later!*

George: *Uh sure! Before you go, can you tell me what needle? Where it is? Why do you need to find it?*

Leader: *It's really important and I don't know exactly where it is, which is why I need you to find it. It's in there somewhere, I just need you to find it.*

George: *Well, can you give me some guidance? Any pointers? How do I approach it? What do I need to complete this task?*

Leader: *I'm sure you can work it out. I don't know how, I just know that it's in there somewhere. Could you please just try and find it for me? It's important.*

The leader goes to the meeting. George will sit in front of the haystack and contemplate numerous options to approach the task. He will likely ask other staff how they would approach the task. In the absence of any other clarity or direction, or understanding of the timeframe that he has to find the needle and why it's so important, George will sit in front of the haystack and start moving a single piece of hay at a time, examining it carefully before discarding it into the 'new' haystack.

George: *That's not it. Nope. That's not it either. No, that's not it.*

The leader comes back two hours later and checks in on George's progress.

Leader: *Hey George, how are you going with that needle?*

George: *It's definitely not in this little pile here! But I'm still looking.*

Frustrated Leader: *Oh George, what happened? Why is it taking you so long?*

George: *Can you give me some direction about where the needle might be?*

Frustrated Leader: *Well, if I knew where it was, I wouldn't need you to find it! I can't believe you have wasted all this time, George. This was really urgent, and you have let me down.*

We can laugh at the silliness of this approach, but these two very different styles often frustrate each other in the workplace. If they have a better understanding of each other's personality, then they might be able to better communicate to address the needs of the other person.

In the absence of clear direction, George can think of no other way to achieve the goal except to sit there and meticulously examine the pieces of hay one by one. The more that the leader resists providing clear guidance and rationale for the task, which would afford George some direction, the more George's anxiety will ensure that he sits there and carefully examines each piece of hay.

Adapting your leadership style for clarity

What George needs from the leader is some understanding about why the needle is there, what the leader needs it for, why it's really important that someone can find the needle in the haystack and for the leader to make some suggestions, such as the following:

Look, George, I know the needle is in there. It's a silver needle and it's essential for tomorrow's board meeting, I have to present that needle to the board, so it's really important that we find it. Why don't you see if you can find a hairdryer and try blowing away some of the hay, that might help speed up the process. I'm thinking that the needle is going to be heavier than the hay and so, theoretically it should be at the bottom somewhere.

George now understands; he knows why he has to find the needle. He knows that there is time pressure, an urgency around it. He also has some ideas about what he can do to try and locate the needle in the haystack. He's less anxious with all of this knowledge and he's more motivated. With a little direction, he can make better progress and the task seems far less daunting. He can think about some other creative ideas that might help — like trying to use a magnet on the thinner pile of hay at the bottom.

When the leader returns a couple of hours later, George has made much more progress, right? He's probably even located the needle! What George needed was direction, but he also needed to be able to understand why his time on this particular task was more important than his other work. With more clarity about the goal, and less confusion about why it was necessary, his chances of success increased, and his time was more productively utilised.

Once George was linked to the strategic outcome that his leader needed help with (that is, once he understood why that needle was needed), his commitment to the success of the task was much stronger. We discuss more about owning outcomes in chapter 5.

As a compassionate leader, the ability to make that connection is where you can really improve communication with the different personality types in your organisation and better utilise their differing skill sets to achieve your goals.

How do supervisors cause psychosocial injuries?

This is a question that I have puzzled over for many years because I have seen some very poor management decisions made by completely reasonable people that were communicated in such a way that they created unreasonable expectations.

Remembering that the biggest cause of a psychosocial injury is poorly managed change, it is essential to be aware that this applies to *any* change — not just big organisational change programs. We continue to see psychosocial injuries in large organisations, despite the fact that managers believe they have consulted with people and communicated the change process. A lot of the time it comes down to different perceptions of the same issue by two people — most often the staff member and their line manager.

The obligation to check on the understanding of any communication is the responsibility of the manager. Perception management is the single most important reason that *all* supervisors must have people management training — but more importantly, people in direct line management roles should be assessed for their empathy. Empathy is an attribute, not a skill that can be learned, as such it is *not* something that every human being exhibits at a consistent level.

Empathy is not the only reason that a line manager will be supportive of a staff member who is having challenges affecting their work, but it affords them a significantly improved ability to not make a strong 'concrete' assessment of the rationale behind a person's behaviour. Concrete thinking is the notion that there are only two assessments of a situation: right or wrong, black or white. If the line manager applies concrete thinking to an assessment of the staff member's motivation or behaviour, this definitive assessment becomes the 'key' to the staff member's outcomes. If they encounter a situation that may impact their ability to make a full contribution to the workplace, an empathic leader will have more compassion and acceptance of the many flexible options in the 'grey' areas, rather than purely black or white.

This is why we talk about the staff member's outcome in any situation being dependent upon the 'leadership lottery'. We must reduce the likelihood that a person's outcome is dependent on chance!

Annette's story

Annette was a young woman with a dream to be a journalist. Although she had worked in the media sector for sometime, nothing had prepared her for the workplace culture she would experience in a large news corporation. The expectation was that she would be available 24/7 and, even if workdays finished at 1 am, she was expected to recommence at 6 am the same day, leaving little time to rest.

In this organisation, most higher-level roles were filled by males, and the junior female levels were given duties more akin to a personal assistant. Menial tasks such as picking up dry cleaning, fetching coffee and paying personal bills were expected, and Annette described the workplace as 'misogynistic' and 'sexist'.

Annette recalls one particularly challenging working relationship with a senior colleague. He had nicknamed her 'Copy', and one day he ordered her to get him a milkshake, to which she responded, 'My name is Annette. My mother taught me to say "please" and "thank you" and some gratitude would really help our relationship.' In response, he yelled, 'I don't care what your fucking name is! Just go and get my fucking milkshake!' Annette was shaken, yet even though there were witnesses to the event, no one intervened. No one stood up for her and challenged the unnecessarily harsh treatment of another human being. No one!

Annette was given an assignment where she needed to interview one of the senior journalists. She attempted to line it up on numerous occasions to no avail, he just ignored her. She required his input to complete her assignment; it couldn't be done without him. Then she happened to run into his secretary one morning, and when she asked about his availability, she was told to go into his office now, that it was a good time.

Annette knocked on the door, entered and said 'Excuse me...' Only to find herself being screamed at with profanities and being told to 'Get out of my fucking office! Who the fuck do you think you are coming in here?' It was so loud that when she went back and sat down at her desk, another colleague looked at her amused and said, 'That didn't go so well, did it?' Her desk was a 100 metres away from his office. She was left upset, without support and without the resources to complete her assignment.

Not only did Annette feel violated as a person, but the lack of support from colleagues who witnessed these daily degrading dialogues, yet did nothing to intervene, was also very isolating. For four years Annette endured this constant verbal barrage, regularly calling out the behaviour with remarks like, 'You can't talk to me like that. I'm not ten, I'm not your child! I'm an adult and this isn't acceptable.'

Unfortunately, the toxic behaviour did not improve, and Annette was extremely frustrated. She was labelled a troublemaker for the occasions she did stand up for herself, and ended up assigned to working on simple administration tasks, despite her writing skills, completely removing her from the role she was hired to do.

After four years Annette had had enough. Annette engaged a solicitor, and attempted to garner some support from her work colleagues, but they were too scared to stand against the status quo. She took the media company to court and was offered an out-of-court settlement of $10 000, but she declined, believing that she would be vindicated in court. However, Annette told me that while the judge acknowledged the bad working conditions, they did not find in her favour as doing so retrospectively would be incredibly damaging for the organisation.

Annette was devastated and unemployed. She took a job was at a publishing house, but after three months they asked her to leave. Annette acknowledges that she was very angry and broken, and that she wasn't performing in the workplace.

Further demoralised, Annette developed a drinking problem and she was smoking marijuana to help her sleep.

The solicitor encouraged her to appeal her claim to a higher court. They even found an outstanding Queens Counsel (QC) who took her on pro bono. They appealed but lost again, sending Annette spiralling into major depression.

Over the next six months Annette became agoraphobic, vomiting when she was forced to leave the house. Her drinking and marijuana consumption increased, and she wasn't eating properly. She lost a lot of weight and her health was very poor. Concerned, a friend kept pushing her to get help, eventually booking an appointment for Annette with a counsellor, and her journey to healing began.

Annette returned to her home town almost 12 months after losing her job. Feeling like a loser, she was ashamed and embarrassed by her feelings of failure. She had left to become a 'big time' journalist, but her dream failed, and instead she returned with feelings of guilt, shame and self-doubt. Annette carried these feelings for years and they impacted all areas of her life. Annette's drug and alcohol abuse continued, along with partying hard and other risky behaviours.

Soon after returning home, Annette found work at a media monitoring service. The work was interesting, but she found the workplace very triggering as the culture was embedded in journalism. She only lasted a year. Annette decided that she no longer wanted to work in media; it had broken her.

Looking for a change, Annette took up a role as a support worker in a supported employment warehouse with 60 people with additional needs. Annette found the role to be cathartic for her, and a place of healing and purpose as she was assisting others to improve their lives. She stayed there for four years.

Annette has always felt like the underdog, fighting to have her voice heard, standing up for justice, what was right and how to treat people. When she was in her really dark place, she would berate herself for not learning to keep her mouth shut. Her new role gave her a voice, and enabled her to support those who were vulnerable. In standing up for their rights, it brought back a sense of self-worth and value.

When I asked Annette what she would like leaders to take away from her experience, she stressed the importance of the duty of care between the employer and a staff member. An organisation has a responsibility to their people to up-skill them for their role — effective training that is adaptive to the mental health and wellbeing of the individual.

Annette believes that access to counselling in high-pressured work environments is essential. Fostering coping skills to manage unrealistic expectations and manage the plethora of personality types, rather than promoting a fiercely competitive workplace. Enabling a formal mentoring process between senior leaders and their staff to enhance strategic insight and engender a feeling of value in your people, will also boost the happiness of any workplace.

Change management is more than just process

Most organisations will experience change at some point, whether it's a merger, acquisition, new product launch or the introduction of a new system. Change can be exciting, but it can also be challenging for employees. The responsibility for effective change rests with good leaders who need to ensure that their team is on board with the changes that are taking place. Compassionate leaders can create buy-in from employees and make the transition smoother for everyone.

Change management is often difficult because it challenges the status quo. Employees may be hesitant to change their ways or adopt new processes. It's important for leaders to explain why change is necessary, especially where there may be a sense of urgency around it. They should also be prepared for resistance from employees and have a plan to overcome it.

Effective change by involving all levels of the organisation

The most effective way to create buy-in from employees is to involve them in the change process. Employees will feel more invested in the change if they understand *why* it is necessary and have a say in how it is implemented.

If you want to ensure buy-in from your people in any change process, you must consult them about the problem

---

Ask your people for their input to ensure they feel heard and engaged in the change management process. This also means taking their concerns into account. When a leader decides that the organisation needs change, they need to approach team members and discuss the problem. Leaders need to outline why there is a problem and highlight that change needs to be made, then ask them for input about a solution.

Many great leaders already know what is needed to resolve the problem and make the change, that's why they're the leader. However, by engaging team members and providing a platform to hear their perspective on what is needed to fix the problem, leaders create 'buy-in' — giving employees a strategic overview and a sense of helping the organisation to resolve a problem.

If your organisation has a hierarchical and structured environment, you may need to implement changes to encourage less formality. Take time to connect with people and talk about some of the challenges, both personal and professional. Acknowledge how these changes have come about and their impact on the organisation, whether they were created by organisational change or not.

Keeping the lines of communication open

Communication is another key factor in change management. In addition to being clear about what changes are taking place and why they are necessary, leaders should also keep employees updated on progress and let them know when things change or if there are any delays. Transparency is crucial during times of change, as it helps to build trust between leaders and employees.

As a leader, you will recognise that chaos results from a variety of internal and external factors, especially where the business has had to pivot. If the organisation needs to go through a period of structural change, you want to minimise the likelihood of creating further chaos by ensuring transparency and effective communication throughout the process.

Tell your team that organisational change is coming. Once the decision for change has been made, leaders should deliver clear and consistent messaging about why the change is necessary, via multiple mediums and across the whole organisation. Many leaders operate on a 'need to know' basis, however, it is good practice to provide broad strategic information to all members of the organisation when change is planned. Such communication should outline how that change process provides the solution for the problem, and how it is actually going to look when rolled out across the organisation.

Depending on the size of the organisation, some changes may be small and may only affect one team. By drawing attention to the issue across the organisation, good leaders demonstrate their effectiveness at solving problems. By highlighting the strategic need to resolve the problem, leaders help employees understand why it's a problem for the business.

Most change management fails because people don't take the time to communicate the problem that the change is actually going to solve. The strategic rationale for the change is not effectively disseminated. Failure to communicate the rationale for change, even if it's only a small change, will result in a lack of support for the rollout of that change. Worse, leaders may experience active resistance to the change.

Change management is a marathon not a sprint

In response to complexity, good leaders will adjust the way that they interact with people. Leaders have become more understanding when people talk about some of their own personal challenges in the workplace and recognise the need for more flexibility. In reality, effectively managing chaos is achieved by unpacking the complexity and creating greater flexibility in the work environment.

A lot of roles are sold to leaders as a 'we really need somebody to come in and hit the ground running' type of role, but hitting the ground running does not mean rapid change. Be comfortable and confident in your ability as a compassionate leader. Good leaders take the time to assess the situation before proposing change. If a change process is rushed it will be met head on with more resistance. If it's a new role for you, take time — at least three months — to settle in before proposing significant change. It takes that long to assess the lay of the land.

When the need for change is understood, the process will happen and be relatively painless. The employees feel that they understand the rationale and they are on board with it.

Why senior leaders need to regularly review their HR data

As organisations grow, they invariably acquire more HR resources. One of the first things I ask senior leaders who are having problems is what is their unplanned personal leave data telling them? The reason that I unpack some of this data is because there are a lot of early warning signs in leave data. Examining the HR data for patterns, like higher rates of unplanned leave in a particular team or periods of higher leave across the organisation following the announcement of a change, can provide us with insight about problems brewing in a particular area of the organisation. When we overlay this data with our standard staff feedback tools, like a staff survey, we get a snapshot of any potential hotspots in your business. If we then layer over the costs of different sectors of the business, we start to formulate a comprehensive early warning system.

As the leader, when you delegate all HR to a HR manager, you increase the risk that you will miss some of the early warning signs. We delegate the management and then we assume they will keep us apprised of any potential issues, but utilising data in this way is not always in the purview of the HR manager. You want to know what's going on with your business, and that includes profits *and* people. Your people are your greatest asset in terms of cost and contribution to your profitability. You want to know if there are any hotspots, as they can indicate challenges with a particular person's management style or that something has changed in that work area, something that otherwise may not be brought to your attention.

It's important to spend some time looking at the data you do capture and work out the elements that will afford you a good snapshot of what is going on in the organisation. Get someone to create a regular report and ensure that you discuss it at your leadership meetings at least once a month. This is also a great tool to ensure your leaders are keeping track of any challenges in their work areas.

Communication needs to be a habit

In most organisations I work with, we can develop some simple traffic light indicators utilising existing data, which will help to prevent psychological injuries from developing. I encourage leaders, regardless of the size of the organisation, to establish regular informal discussion forums with people from varying levels within the business. Mix it up so that you're getting different perspectives over time. It's essential that these discussions are 'frank and fearless', and that requires some assurance of confidentiality — the 'cone of silence' needs to be respected. Nothing that is discussed in these 'pulse check' opportunities are taken out and used against anybody. This is essential to the success of the process, because you need to build a sense of trust within your people. They need to know that they can speak openly about something and how it makes them feel, without it coming back to bite them.

The benefit of an independent review

I find that many organisations get caught in a 'replacement' culture when it comes to recruitment. Most organisations that I work with will perform some level of skills audit of their people. This is something that should also be built in as part of your mentoring and development program. There should be a regular reassessment of the work distribution, and, periodically, you should engage a consultant to undertake an independent review of your processes. Sometimes it's really useful to have an independent, yet curious, mind to review your business.

If an external consultant is outside your budget, I suggest that you implement a 'bring your four-year-old to work' day! By that, I mean that you instruct your staff to come to work and cross-reference each other's business processes by asking the age-old, very annoying question: *'But why?'* In this way, we can support each other to continuously improve our ways of doing things and build in a tolerance for scrutiny. We have to value opportunities for improvement by creatively building them into our workplace.

The stumbling block for most organisations is that they don't place any value on the corporate resources, with the exception of finances. HR is perceived to solely focus on entitlements, policy and payroll, with minimal interest in employee wellbeing. Any focus on wellbeing is often focused on physical health, rather than mental health — and there is little awareness of holistic health encompassing both aspects. But, the emergence of the chief mental health officer role is starting to gain momentum, and I think all medium-sized enterprises (over 100 staff) need a 'Chief Happiness Officer'.

Spotting early signs of a negative change in culture

There are certain behaviours and activities that lead some sectors to develop really toxic work environments. You don't want a toxic work environment. You don't want anybody to come in and create one. So, you need to keep your finger on the pulse of the business — your people. If you are getting mixed messages from one area of the business and you feel like you are missing something, the manager may not be giving you full insight into what is happening. As the leader of your organisation, it's your job to find out what is really going on. I recognise that, as leaders, you are really busy, but it's essential that you don't just accept the perspective that you are given by one manager. If you do, you often have to deal with a much bigger problem later. At worst, we can uncover something that was brewing that you just didn't notice was there!

Ultimately, you are working towards building a self-managing business. You are creating systems that identify any potential hazards and regularly review and mitigate risks, and developing teams that are solutions focused rather than problem focused. If you notice that you currently have a problem-focused team, then you need to proactively change your approach to decision-making. Problem-focused teams haven't been empowered by their leader to develop creative solutions to the problems that they come across. Once you have truly empowered your people, they will outline a problem to you and proffer a number of solutions for you to choose from.

CHAPTER 4

Conscientious Leadership

How to foster it in the workplace

Whether we are talking about emotional intelligence, empathy or soul-centred leadership, we are focusing on the notion that we bring our whole sense of care and concern to our decision-making as a leader. In this way, we promote an environment of emotional safety in the workplace.

I often find this notion tends to 'bristle' leaders in Western corporates. In fact, when I look back at some of the corporate thought leaders from the last 50 years, I see deliberate action to avoid any emotional presence in the workplace — unless it was used to gain some an advantage over a competitor or client.

Mark H McCormack's book *What they don't teach you at Harvard Business School*[17] promotes the use of psychological principles to gain an advantage over your competitors, negotiate deals and control employees. This incredibly popular book was written at a time when business deals were made on the golf course, and the key communication tool in business was a well-worded letter on important-looking letterhead! Is it really any surprise that this insular system has given way to poor health outcomes via chronic disease and heart failure?

The changing world of work

One of the big shifts that resulted from COVID-19 was that employees really pulled back from the system of work, and had time to reflect on what was important to them — perhaps it was their families or their ability to live a life they enjoyed, which also means having the freedom to do that. We have heard many people talk about the 'Great Resignation' (as discussed in chapter 1), and the corporate world now needs to contend with digital nomads in ways that we never thought possible.

With the advancement of technology, we can automate various processes in our business systems; however, the roles that deliver human services are not easily replaced with technology. Elements of each role can be streamlined, but we are a long way from eliminating human resources completely. Despite this, many organisations don't really value the cost of training an employee or the cost of replacing them.

I see many and varied approaches to leadership, from real empathy to concrete distancing — largely this is reflective of the value that you place on your people. I find the leadership approach seems to take the 'life' out of it; there is often a distance in the decision-making that is not reflective of the fact that we are dealing with living, breathing human beings. I liken it to the way that the Family Court tends to view pets in a family dispute, which is as chattels rather than living beings. Many organisations also tend to think of their people as chattels that can easily be replaced at a moderate cost to the business. Yet, the human element of business costs us so much more than mere training.

Unhappy employees are less productive, less creative and less likely to take initiative. This results in higher unplanned leave and higher turnover.[18] It really does pay to foster conscientious leadership in yourself and your team.

So how do leaders do this? In chapter 3 I talked about leadership as a trait that can't be learned, but can be fostered. Management is a skill, and it can be learned. Many leaders can consciously improve their leadership capabilities, and one of the greatest ways to improve is through reflection and conscious attention.

Consciously leading

How often have you turned up to work so stressed that you feel like you can't take the time to stop because you have so much to do? I understand how this feels, especially when you work in a reactive work environment. However, recognising your own stress levels is essential to your ability to develop conscientious leadership skills.

Many leaders wait until they are overwhelmed with the pressures of the workplace before they reach out for assistance. If you are reading these words and nodding your head, it's a good sign that even if you are feeling the pressure of your workplace, it hasn't yet tipped into chaos. So, how can you foster your self-awareness in the midst of pressure?

One of the best ways to focus on your self-awareness is to step back from the pressured environment for a short period, and decide to become aware of yourself as a conscious leader.

We all know a person who seems to have zero self-awareness in the workplace. The process of therapy supports people to develop better self-awareness, and while I'm not saying that every leader requires therapy, the belief that you wouldn't derive any benefit from it is usually indicative of a person who lacks self-awareness.

Yes, I do expect that some people will want to stop reading now. However, I challenge you to reflect on your reaction to this statement, as it's a good indication that you have had an emotional reaction, and this is the biggest indicator that something is being repressed.

Self-examination is the hardest process that we can undertake as human beings, primarily because it gives rise to a variety of negative beliefs that we have spent our life trying to repress, because we don't know how to process them.

Taking a long hard look at ourselves to achieve self-awareness is extremely uncomfortable — most people avoid it

---

When trying to resolve the challenges of leading your organisation, recognise that you need to do some self-examination. Surprise! You thought this book was going to be about how you fix everyone else, but I am going to challenge you to 'fit your own mask first'!

This has two purposes: it will help you to understand yourself and your own motivations, and it will support you to increase your empathy. So, throughout this chapter, I am going to focus on how you develop a better understanding of yourself, your self-management system and how that shows up in your life, and then I am going to show you how to apply that to your work context.

The self-management system

For a more comprehensive explanation of the underlying principles of how the self-management system develops, I would encourage you to read my book *The Trouble With Trauma*. This book dives into your own challenges more deeply, but for the purposes of the workplace, I want to focus on understanding your own Self-Management System (SMS) and how to utilise this at work.

Conscious leaders can use this system to ground their staff in their SMS when there is a situation that activates emotion in the workplace. By understanding this system and training teams in unpacking their own SMS, organisations are better able to diffuse any emotionally loaded situation in the workplace. Let's look at this in more detail.

We all have parts

Many of you may have heard of internal family systems, archetypes or other terms to describe the varied ways our personality shows up in the world. I'm going to provide a really brief overview about how to understand our parts, and how this helps us understand ourselves and our staff in the work environment.

As you can see in figure 4.1, our SMS is defined by four main parts: child, protector, numb and rational. We also break down the four areas of the system into a further three states. This enables us to distance ourselves a little from the emotional experience and allows us to become a curious observer of our behaviour, rather than caught in the behaviour, unable to change anything or stop it from being expressed. Let's look at how this works.

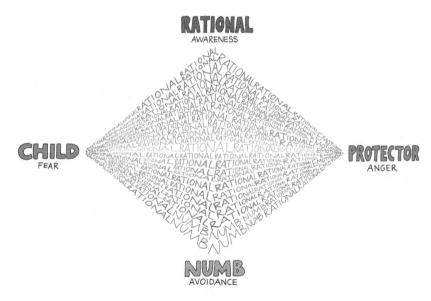

Figure 4.1: The Self-Management System

How our parts show up in our life

In essence, when we are experiencing any obvious emotion, we have tapped into either our child or protector parts. These appear as behaviours in all areas of life, and they show up when we have been emotionally triggered. All big emotional reactions are either child parts, which is our expression of fear and sadness, or protector parts, which is our expression of anger and frustration.

When we are unable to get what we want or need from our expression of emotion, we move into our numb parts, which is where we avoid the feelings by engaging in some addictive activity. This is how we cope with things we can't change, but don't want to address.

In order to live a happy and fulfilling life, we need to spend the majority of our waking hours in our rational parts, where we can feel calm, happy and fulfilled. It's our rational adult self that is reading this book, and thinking about what we want for ourselves and how to get it.

The goal is to become more aware of the different parts in our own system, and how we become triggered. Then we recognise the emotional reaction and develop the self-awareness to catch it before we react emotionally. Over time, we improve our capacity to be aware of the emotional reaction, and use that to stop ourselves acting on it. This enables us to develop a stronger internal checking system about what triggers our emotional reactivity, and intervene before we behave badly.

It is important to understand that we all have both child and protector parts of our self that are responsible for our negative emotional expressions. Depending on our upbringing, when we experience strong negative emotions, we respond consistently and automatically as either protector or child, and we flip between the two. Even if we don't express the emotion in behaviour, we still need to build awareness of the emotional reactivity.

Mapping our parts

Whether I am working with an individual or a team, I find it helpful to unpack their SMS into a map of their parts to help them to understand which part is activated when they are triggered in the workplace (see figure 4.2, overleaf). This supports them to understand their own emotional reactions, and it enables the team to recognise their colleagues' potential triggers whenever there is conflict in the workplace.

The goal of this exercise in self-awareness is to provide some clarity around our interactions in the workplace and to help us understand our own behaviour and the behaviour of others. The goal of building self-awareness utilising the SMS is to recognise when we are activated in negative emotion (our child or protector parts), and seek to move towards our rational parts rather than our numb parts. We want to move forward towards the resolution of any conflict, rather than remaining avoidant.

We will unpack this in detail shortly, but in general in the workplace, we hope to see the rational parts (worker, seeker and socialite) interacting with others most of the time. This means that we are generally relaxed and happy, focused and engaged. If there is any conflict in the workplace, we hope to see the positive protector and child parts: assertive and good child. These are the parts that operate more proactively to find a solution and maintain cohesiveness.

In essence, we rarely see our most extreme negative child or protector parts in the workplace, unless it's a toxic workplace. Aggressive, passive aggressive and alone child are often present in dysfunctional environments. Baby state is usually only seen in the safety of our home, but might show up regularly if your workplace is toxic.

Child parts

Good child: needs to be needed

This is the part of the self that we activate when we feel rejected, and we are trying to repair a connection with another person: the feeling that I need to do something nice to make that person like me again.

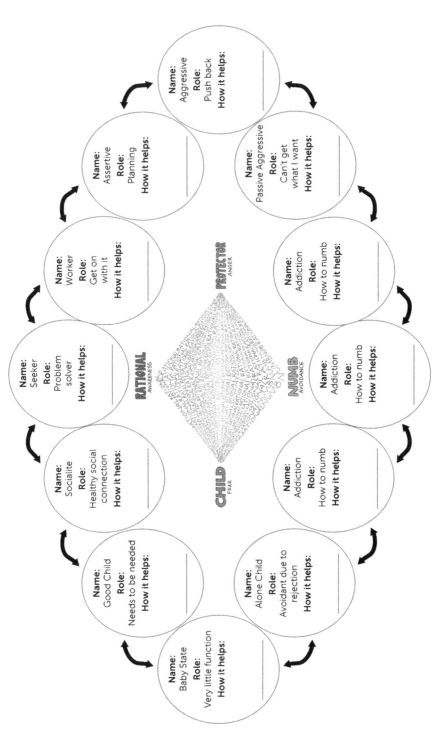

Figure 4.2: Unpacking your self-management system

How it helps: This is the state that we move into when we are moving away from isolation (see baby state or alone child), but feeling positive and seeking connection. It is from this aspect of self that we try and engage another person in a reconnection. It's our 'nice' part who wants to be friends again.

Alone child: stays alone fearing rejection

When we are fearing further rejection, this is the part of self that we see in action. The feeling that I should just stay away from others and keep to myself.

How it helps: We see this state when we are moving away from complete isolation (baby state), but still feel negative and withdrawn. It's often from this aspect of self that we slip into diverting our attention with our numb parts, so that we can avoid the shame of feeling rejected.

Baby state: very little functioning

We activate this state when we are most withdrawn. The feeling that we get when we have ended a relationship or are feeling rejected at work, and we just want to pull the doona over our head.

How it helps: This is a biologically activated protective state that is activated by your vagus nerve. At our most withdrawn, we are taking the time to calm our central nervous system. In the 'fight, flight, freeze' activation, this goes one step further to 'collapse'.

Protector parts

Assertive: advocate/planner

This is the part of self that we activate when we feel unfairly treated and we are seeking to resolve the disconnection with another person. The feeling that I need to stand up for myself, but I'm trying to find a solution.

How it helps: It resolves conflict. This is the part of the self that we activate when we have disagreed with someone, but we feel clear on what's right, and we are prepared to resolve the conflict through discussion.

Passive aggressive: stonewalled

If we feel we have been unfairly treated and we can't get what we want to resolve the disconnection with the other person, we find ourself in this state. It's the feeling that there is no point in trying to have a discussion.

How it helps: By being quietly protective, this state helps us when we feel unable to resolve the conflict for some reason. We maintain the frustration but withdraw as we feel like there is no point in discussing it.

Aggressive: push back

We activate this part in anger when we feel unfairly treated and we are asserting our position, regardless of the potential threat of disconnection with the other person. The feeling that I need to defend my position regardless of the outcome.

How it helps: This is our strongest defender; the part that we activate as a trigger response to a sense of unfairness or injustice. It asserts our position clearly regardless of the consequences.

Numb parts

Addiction: avoidance

These are the parts of self that we activate when we feel that resolution is not attainable. The feeling that we need to divert away from our feelings because we can't resolve them. They are different for everyone, so only you know which activities you turn to when you can't get what you want. This could be any number of addictive behaviours, such as alcohol, eating, pornography, shopping, or avoidance behaviour like sleeping.

How they help: This behaviour enables our brain to focus on something else by activating a different emotional state based on the activity.

Rational parts

Socialite: healthy connector

This is the part of self that we activate when we are feeling generally happy and wanting to engage socially with others. The feeling that I want to connect with people because it brings me joy.

How it helps: This state ensures that we maintain bonds so we feel connected, and it provides us with a sense of community. Connection is essential to our survival and this part is responsible for ensuring that this is done well.

Worker: focused

This state is activated when we are focused and functioning well. We can make plans and see them through. The feeling that I have clear goals and I can work to achieve them.

How it helps: When we are in this state, it enables us to feel that we have value, both in the workplace and around our family and friends. It's the ability to feel accomplished and proud of ourselves for our achievements.

Seeker: problem solver

This is the part of self that we activate when we find ourselves unable to achieve a goal and we are looking for answers. The feeling that I need to research options or seek advice to find a solution.

How it helps: The problem solver state enables you to focus your attention on finding solutions to your challenges. Your seeker is the part reading this book!

* * *

We need to understand ourselves in all of our relationships and our connections with other human beings and where we are coming from in that interaction. If we are reacting to someone in hurt or anger, we have usually perceived a potential rejection; we feel that we are going to be abandoned. Our clarity and understanding of ourselves and our own feelings is fundamentally important, because in any interpersonal connection that we have, we have to understand ourselves and how we react, so we can communicate to the other person why we reacted the way we did.

When we develop self-awareness and better understand ourselves, we can own our feelings and manage our behaviour, through more effective and honest communication about our needs.

Part III

Risk and Psychological Safety

CHAPTER 5

Validation
Judgement vs acknowledgement

When I talk about 'validation', a lot of people get confused by what I am actually referring to. If we look at the definition of 'validation', we find two distinct definitions of validation.

the action of checking or proving the validity or accuracy of something, in some cases to declare something legally or officially acceptable

which is distinctly different to:

recognition or affirmation that a person or their feelings or opinions are valid or worthwhile.

I believe that it is in this distinction of action (judgement) vs recognition (acknowledgement) that the meaning of validation has become confused in the English language. We need to separate them if we want to support psychological safety in the workplace.

How our brains process trauma

When we experience a traumatic event, regardless of the event, there are two scenarios that determine whether or not it will be 'filed' as traumatic in our brains: our sense of direct responsibility for the event outcome *or* our sense of feeling powerless to prevent its impact.

The act of validation, by its dual nature, can therefore determine through 'action' the 'recognition' of the feelings experienced by an individual in any situation. The validation of our perception of any given situation is important to our ability to appropriately process the information into our memory network.

It is a natural part of our human experience that we look to others to confirm our perceptions of experience. In this way, humans learn to assess their own perceptions and judgements against those of our peers. It is a normal part of the human experience to model ourselves on those whom we respect, and to distance ourselves from those who we don't feel aligned with on a wide variety of issues. At the most basic level, it informs group dynamics and social theories of group development.[19] This is the basis of all human psychology, as it is our need to maintain connection with other human beings that shapes our ability to feel safe and secure, and ultimately to sustain life.

It should come as no surprise, then, that we find ourselves retelling our experiences in work and life to those we admire in an unconscious effort to validate our perception of the experiences.

Connection to other human beings is essential to our perception of psychological safety

---

Telling stories

You won't really be surprised to learn that telling stories is an important part of how we process emotionally laden and stored material. Our experiences are perceived and assessed, and if they evoke significant emotional responses, this is a 'trigger' to mark the experience as one that needs to be validated. We then seek out colleagues and friends to whom we re-tell the story, often embellished with stronger emotional expression than we expressed at the time. By engaging in this social ritual, we are able to either obtain a consensus that our feelings are appropriate and validated, or we experience a psychological phenomenon that causes us further distress because we are unable to obtain validation of our perceived experience.

Storytelling has psychological benefits

The act of storytelling has a number of psychological benefits that have been well documented in literature and multiple research studies. The narrative is related to adaptive psychological functioning, so the telling of the story is important. Without stories, the memory becomes stuck or frozen, unable to be processed.[20] Without effective memory recall, we cannot imagine how things could be different.[21, 22]

You may be surprised to learn that children begin to create stories about events in their lives before the age of three.[23, 24] Not surprisingly, stories enable a child to make sense of the world and form a fundamental building block in helping a child become psychologically integrated. By the time most children start school, they are able to create their own narratives, even recognising story structure (that there is a beginning, middle and end). They expect a resolution to the plot complications that develop over the course of a story.[25]

We gain a sense of purpose in our lives through the construction of narratives. Stories support us to organise and act on desires to accomplish our goals.[25] Telling stories to others to seek validation helps us reach a point where the memory can be adaptively stored.

In this way, we can understand how the ability to provide recognition validation for an individual's perception of an experience can really support them to develop a different narrative about it. As human beings, we don't always need to agree, but we do need to feel heard to move forward.

Storytelling isn't just something that we do for entertainment purposes; it is an essential component to our appropriate emotional processing of the experience. Through retelling the story, with the addition of our feelings and experiences about the actions, we are able to obtain social validation of our experiences.

At least that is what we HOPE for...

Storytelling is an essential component of our ability to process emotional experiences

---

What happens when we're not validated?

Invalidation is so common in the modern workplace that we have adopted social constructs that enable us to process it — and you just thought it was office gossip! You will notice this in certain environments where a staff member has a negative experience with a colleague or supervisor, and they spend the rest of the afternoon 'gossiping' (repeating the story) to colleagues or on the phone to family and friends seeking support for their perception of the experience. Whether or not they receive support will impact their ability to either process their memory in an appropriate manner, or not.

When the person finds validation both inside and outside of the organisation of their perception, they tend to feel validated to take action. Depending on the issue, this may mean anything from initiating a discussion with the colleague that they had the problem with, to lodging a formal complaint. In essence, they feel validated in their perception and will likely take some action to express their position because they perceive that their assessment is correct.

Sometimes the validation is obtained from outside of the organisation (family or friends), but not from inside the organisation (colleagues). When this happens, depending on the size of the problem, the person may feel targeted by members of the organisation. This is the most risky validation process because it is not 'filtered' by the organisational context. The validation by friends and family may be based on the biased retelling of the story — something that humans naturally do to make their perspective stronger.

If a person is invalidated both inside and outside the organisation, they may feel sad, but they will usually process things reasonably quickly and accept that they were wrong. They may then make changes, or not, but they will usually move forward.

Why we need to validate

It is important to understand that we need to provide validation through recognition of the person's perception of the experience, not necessarily through the action of validation. We may need to provide empathy for the person's perspective, without taking responsibility for following an action to validate it — therefore, without judgement.

Sorry is NOT the admission of liability, it is the acknowledgement of another person's pain

---

This is where judgement can create a lot of challenges in the workplace. We spend too much time focused on the 'action' of validation before we consider the 'recognition' of it. Yet, it is recognition validation that will enable us to feel comfortable, even in the absence of action validation.

You will understand the feeling that I am describing when you think back to a time when you told a story about something negative that happened to you, and the person that you were telling your story to says 'I'm sorry about that', and you immediately respond with 'No need to apologise!' In this interaction, you are responding to the expression of empathy from a person who wasn't involved in your distress, yet they show you some emotional recognition of your pain. We are so conditioned to only accept empathy from the source of the pain that we tend to downplay empathy from any other source, as it feels uncomfortable.

As human beings, we have an inbuilt barometer of emotional regulation as a result of both our inherent nature and our experience in our nurturing environments. We are almost a human scale that seeks to 'balance' the positive and negative emotions that we hold at any given time. When someone adds something significant to the 'negative' scale, the balancing item has to be of equal value. Ideally, this would be where the person who added the item to the negative scale chooses to remove it. Without this, you need a larger proportion of effort from others to acknowledge the negative experience to 'lighten the load'.

Ideally, if you are the source of an event that is negatively perceived by another person, the greatest gain is achieved when you acknowledge their pain. We can do this without removing the judgement of the action, assuming that the action was a reasonable and appropriate one.

Validation facilitates recovery

The mere act of validation of a person's perception is usually enough to completely change their attitude about it. I am basing this on single episodes, as it is much easier to provide validation at each step of the process than to try and resolve the cumulative impacts of a conflict that has built over several episodes of invalidation.

When I provide mediation services in an organisation, or when I am training and mentoring a mediation approach into a corporate structure, the mere act of communicating validation is key to resolving most issues and achieving consensus. The key to facilitating communication is being able to ensure that both parties feel heard.

As human beings, we tend to naturally seek to defend ourselves from perceptions of negativity. Allowing a person to express their issues in a negative way makes every human feel like they have to express their own perspective. Depending on how the negative perception is communicated, we can feel like we are under attack. The issue is that then we immediately jump to defence at the first sign of a negatively expressed view.

In essence, we stop listening.

Mediation facilitates being heard

The process of mediation is defined as 'a process wherein the parties meet with a mutually selected impartial and neutral person who assists them in the negotiation of their differences'. When I work with organisations where a toxic culture has developed, one of the first things I do is train the middle managers in simple mediation techniques, and set up an internal system whereby the mediation process is first facilitated internally before being escalated to an external provider.

This provides the organisation with several elements of capability. It not only supports middle managers to behave in a neutral manner, but encourages them to examine information from both sides, without judgement, and coach the parties to a resolution. In performing these roles for different areas within the corporation, managers are provided with insight into the challenges experienced by other managers and team members within other areas of the business, but in such a way that they start to broaden their perspectives. It affords the organisation a win–win resolution by improving the people skills of middle managers and reducing the likelihood of unreasonable behaviour getting out of hand.

Some see the act of mediation as just a form of negotiation — this is how mediation operates within a court process. In such a process, the mediator facilitates the telling of the story by both parties, and then separates them to try and negotiate a resolution by going back and forth between the parties to reach a compromise. In some cases, the mediator will place pressure on the parties to move them closer to a compromise.

There is nothing more powerful than being heard to overcome the sense of feeling invalidated

However, in a business environment we need to view mediation as the role of 'curious observer'. This role is about taking the time to hear both perspectives, and utilising communication skills and reflective listening techniques to facilitate a resolution through coaching. This is not about putting pressure on either party; rather it's about building active listening skills to reframe perspectives and provide validation of the experience of both parties. It's a very powerful tool to enhance the interpersonal skills of your middle management.

If we reflect back to what I said at the beginning of this chapter about the process of seeking validation through storytelling, you can imagine how powerful it is to feel heard by the person that you felt invalidated by.

Case study: Monica

Monica is a full-time team leader who works for a government department and has done so for over a decade. She has an exemplary work record and manages a small team, including some staff with significant mental health challenges. Monica is empathetic and supportive as a team leader, committed to her work and effective in her role.

Monica is an immigrant and her extended family still live overseas. Her uncle died suddenly and as they are Orthodox, the burial must occur within three days. Monica's family are the only family members and she must organise flights for herself and her parents to immediately go overseas, tend to the funeral arrangements and sort his affairs.

This is a sudden and unexpected situation that Monica's workplace is not prepared for. Monica advises her manager as soon as she finds out, and explains that she must accompany her parents overseas to bury her uncle, as their religion requires. She keeps her manager in the loop via text message over the weekend about their plans.

At the airport, Monica is engaged in a text conversation with her manager about her leave entitlements — the manager insists that she must submit her leave request electronically before she leaves the country. As the government technical system is very secure, Monica would need to access the system via her work computer, which she has (quite rightly) left at home. The manager doesn't really acknowledge Monica's feelings, but remains focused on Monica's entitlements and steadfast in their insistence that Monica is required to act on things before she leaves the country — something that is actually not in line with HR procedures. Monica emails her manager while she is on leave to explain her family obligations; however, the manager refuses to acknowledge the explanation, choosing to rigidly focus on Monica's leave entitlements.

Not surprisingly, this creates a rift between Monica and her manager. When Monica returns to work several weeks later to discover that the manager hasn't progressed any of her work, preferring to blame Monica for the lack of progress. Not once does the manager express sympathy for her loss. Monica takes more time off because she is feeling so distressed about the way her manager had been treating her. When Monica contacts HR, they confirm that the manager's approach to her leave was incorrect, so the feelings of being unsupported are compounded.

When Monica returns to work wearing black (religious obligations require this as a sign of respect in grief), her attire is commented on as 'dreary and dull', despite it being appropriate business attire. Overall, Monica not only feels unsupported by the manager, but she is now feeling targeted and persecuted for her family situation and religious obligations.

Not surprisingly, Monica decides that she doesn't want to work with this manager anymore and proceeds to actively look for another role. The lack of trust that has now developed as a result of this situation has led to Monica choosing to use other referees for her job seeking, so the manager isn't aware that she is planning to leave. In addition, Monica is no longer focused on progressing her work as she has already mentally left the role, so the manager is becoming more frustrated with Monica and starts telling others that she is 'not performing'.

When Monica is offered another position, the manager tries to enforce the longest possible notice period in an attempt to further punish Monica for her perceived abandonment. So, Monica's general practitioner provides her with a medical certificate for excessive stress, which covers her for the remainder of her notice period.

Sound familiar?

Resolution: Monica

When we consider Monica's circumstances, I want to highlight several opportunities for the manager to have provided recognition validation, even if they didn't want to provide action validation. In this case, action validation should have also been provided to Monica.

Opportunity #1: Good people don't replace good processes

If the team had a good system for tracking work progress (including due dates, required input, people responsible, etc.), then the manager would have had immediate insight into the status of Monica's work. The first issue here is that the manager had become too reliant on Monica's good work ethic, and had stopped maintaining high-level oversight of the work due to Monica's effectiveness.

Action: Ensure that you have a system to track work, and that you regularly receive high-level updates on the work that your team leaders are progressing. Inform them that it is not about micro-managing (it really isn't), it's about supporting the progress of urgent work if there is an unexpected event.

Opportunity #2: We all have trigger points, be aware of yours

Next, we note that the manager became focused on Monica's obligations to comply with leave requests, narrowing their focus on her, in an attempt to control her actions.

Action: Note the tendency within yourself to become frustrated in situations that cause stress. Try to note any frustration within yourself about the impact of a person's actions on your workload, as this is usually the impetus for retaliating by exerting your power.

As a manager, it is your obligation to check yourself when you feel the need to enforce rules with one of your staff members. Ask yourself, 'why am I so angry with them?' Once you identify your frustration, you can problem solve the solution. Building this level of self-awareness is essential if you want to become a great leader, rather than just an efficient manager.

Opportunity #3: Acknowledge the other perspective

Monica responds to the feeling of being pressured by emailing her manager, by way of explanation and in an attempt to achieve some resolution.

Action: If your staff member is reaching out to explain their circumstances, take the time to acknowledge their perspective, even if you don't agree with it — it's still their perspective and it deserves to be respected and acknowledged. Just acknowledge the pain expressed by the employee and avoid all attempts to 'counter' it by expressing your own pain (such as having to take on the extra work).

Opportunity #4: Communicate and support the rest of your team

While Monica is on leave, the manager doesn't finalise any of her work and blames her for the failure to deliver. Monica returns to a long list of demands from different areas of the organisation requiring urgent action. The team has also not been managed in her absence and Monica is expected to 'sign off' on timesheets and other team leader responsibilities for her team members for periods that she was not supervising.

Action: The manager should have communicated openly with other sections of the business that Monica had to take immediate leave due to an emergency family situation. By asking other departments who are working with your absent team member to consider delaying progress until they return (if not urgent) or to contact the manager directly (if urgent), you give other departments a clear path to continue to meet their goals. Communicate that 'work will continue' but everyone will need to carry a little bit of the extra load to support the team member until they return. Express empathy for their circumstance and reinforce the fact that the team needs to focus on the urgent and important work, to ensure the person is not overwhelmed upon their return.

Opportunity #5: Embrace diversity as an organisational strength

Monica returns from leave and is following her cultural obligations in her dress. This is met with negative comments.

Action: The manager should have discussed Monica's trip with her and taken the time to listen to the challenges she experienced. They should have expressed sympathy for her loss. Monica should have been asked if she would like to communicate anything to the broader group about her cultural obligations, so that they understand why she is wearing black. The manager should have taken the time to regularly check in with Monica and just ask how she is feeling and if there is anything that she needs help with.

The remainder of the scenario is not going to happen now, because the manager has altered their approach using the tips here. As a result, Monica will eventually return to her former capacity in the coming weeks, and she will feel so supported by her work area that she will feel a sense of loyalty to the manager and her fellow team members for providing support to her during a time of tremendous personal distress. This saves the work area time and money in lost productivity from Monica mentally disengaging, but also in the need to recruit and train a new team leader.

Leadership stress

I have heard many of these types of stories and I often have tried to understand what is going through the mind of the manager in this scenario. Monica is the most reliable team leader in her section, so why would you be so rigid in your approach?

The most likely answer is that Monica's sudden departure is going to place pressure on the manager to step in and manage Monica's team in her absence — in addition to everything else that the manager has to do. Now, all of a sudden, we can start to see why Monica's manager is feeling very stressed about what her sudden departure will mean for the work that has to be finalised while Monica is away. In this case, the absence is likely to be several weeks, and there is no opportunity to plan ahead to find someone to backfill Monica's position.

114

The approach that the manager takes at this point is going to depend on how stressed the manager is: the greater the pressure, the more likely the manager is to focus their frustration on the source of the most significant stressor — Monica.

The attitude of the manager is also mediated by their perception of Monica's family circumstances. They are from different cultural backgrounds and have different obligations to family. The manager appears to personally disagree with Monica's obligations and feels abandoned by her. As such, the manager makes a negative action validation about Monica's circumstances, and begins to utilise all of their power as line manager to make the situation difficult for her.

Provide recognition validation without action validation

This is something that leaders struggle with because it seems counterintuitive. The easiest way to think about it is that it is learning to express empathy for how the unhappy staff member feels about the disagreement, without assessing the subject of the conflict.

Reflect back to what I said earlier about how we feel when someone says that they are 'sorry' for a situation that they played no part in. This is the same phenomenon, but it can be challenging to express because usually, as the leader, you were part of the situation. However, it takes great self-awareness and skill as a conscientious leader to develop the ability to acknowledge another person's pain without taking responsibility for it.

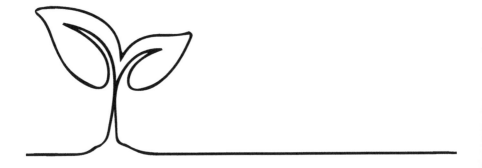

CHAPTER 6

Mitigating Risk in Psychological Safety

Know the situations that put your staff at risk

When we consider the interpersonal issues that can create psychological challenges in the workplace, we should start by looking at time. Many claims for workplace psychological injury come within three months of a change. There are valid reasons why this is common in this timeframe, which I will expand on in chapter 8, but it helps to understand how this is a significant key in potentially achieving a 'quick win' in your workplace.

Understanding how psychosocial hazards link together is essential to understanding why this time period is such a significant risk point.

There are a number of situations that can put your staff at risk of psychological harm. While not all change comes from recruitment of new staff to an organisation, this is a great starting point to explore reducing the risk.

Onboarding

When you have a new staff member join your organisation, what processes are they taken through to introduce them to your organisation, their roles and responsibilities, and their key deliverables? What about who they report to and what they should do if they are feeling unsure, confused, overwhelmed or lost?

Depending on the size of your organisation, you may have a dedicated team of HR people who are responsible for familiarising new employees with the work environment, or it may be left to a peer performing a similar role. If the latter, this can be problematic because you have probably recruited because you need more hands on deck, and the peer is usually so busy trying to get everything done that they throw piecemeal work at the new employee. This has the effect of making the new person feel that they are just being given all the work that existing employees don't want to do.

The induction of a new employee in a consistent and replicable manner is essential to ensuring that the new employee understands their role, their deliverables and their reporting lines, as well as being introduced to the equipment that they have to work with and ensuring that it is suited to their personal needs. Then they need to know who to go to when they have questions (they will have many), and that contact person needs to be carefully selected to ensure that they make the new employee feel supported. Too often we recruit into already overwhelmed working environments where we throw a new employee into the deep end and expect them to 'sink or swim'.

As more Gen Z enter the work environment, we see that the sink or swim approach has created higher levels of staff turnover and higher rates of dissatisfaction. There are many complex societal and psychological reasons that Gen Z's approach to work is very different to earlier generations, but it is different. Their general sense of self is built on a very fragile ego base thanks to their life being externalised on social media platforms. They have extremely high levels of mental health literacy but lack resilience. Due to the fact that their busy working parents were too time poor to enforce learning, they lack the problem-solving skills to overcome challenges. They are the generation of learned helplessness combined with egocentricity that results in the perception that everyone else is responsible for their dissatisfaction — in life and work.

As a society, this will be a challenge for future generations, especially on the back of the next generation of pandemic-inspired anxieties. Suffice to say it is essential that we adapt our work environments to ensure we provide adequate provision for building resilience in our young workforce, and this takes time and patience.

To support onboarding, we require clear and consistent documentation, supported by video instruction (essential for younger generations) and a clear explanation of how the quality of work is established, rather than assessed. When we utilise the assessment approach, it appears personal, so setting parameters that can be benchmarked to determine quality is important. Thankfully, even in qualitative fields, we can utilise technology to determine success of the work output. The less personal assessment that we overlay onto a role, the less likely we are to have a perception issue that feels 'personal'.

For many of you, what I am describing is going to feel like a lot of work, and it can be really challenging to step back and distil a process into its benchmarkable elements when you have been doing the job for a long time. When I am working with an organisation in crisis, we prioritise the assessment of standard operating procedures (SOPs) very early in the project because it often provides a quick win in terms of identifying some of the simplest hazards. Regularly reviewing SOPs is also important, as organisational growth and new technology developments will quickly change the way we work.

Humans are really simple animals who thrive on homeostasis — we like certainty. This is especially true when we are on a steep learning curve, like starting a new role. There is a delicate balance between getting someone new up to speed and overwhelming them. Getting the balance right is something that can be readily determined through reflective listening. Some people are very quick to pick things up and others need repetition; learning styles are as different as individuals and have no correlation to intelligence.

People thrive in homeostasis — the ability to remain stable — humans like certainty

---

All new situations activate a level of anxiety in people, and while small levels of anxiety are needed to produce positive actions, too much can be overwhelming. In psychological terms, we talk about the 'window of tolerance': the sweet spot of being aroused enough to be engaged but not hyper-aroused. Good communication with your new starter should enable you to determine their anxiety levels and communicate to them that you understand that their anxiety is normal and you want to help them manage it.

New leadership

When new leadership is brought into an organisation or a team, it alters the dynamics of the team. Good leaders will take their time to ease into a new area and get to know their new team members. However, on occasion, a person has been recruited because of issues with the previous management, and they are given a directive from the hierarchy that isn't necessarily communicated to the team. This will always cause challenges in the workplace.

I am regularly called in by a new CEO about four months into their role. The main reason is usually because the board of directors have given the new CEO a task, but they don't want the staff to be made aware of the issues. However, people are not mushrooms. If you don't provide them with the reality of the situation, then they will tend to make it up!

When a corporate has been poorly managed, to the extent that a leadership change is necessary, the expectation is often that the new leader should turn around the difficulties, but do it without airing all of the organisation's dirty laundry! There are many reasons for this: from fears around litigation for potential slander, through to the board's embarrassment that the business was failing right under their noses. Regardless of the rationale for not telling staff the truth about previous business failings, it is never a good idea to try and sweep things under the rug.

The most inclusive thing that a new leader can do is be open about the problems, and ask their new teams what needs to be done to fix it. This rarely happens, not just because the hierarchy may have told the new CEO not to disclose the problems, but usually because the CEO wants to be viewed as the 'fountain of knowledge' — after all, that is why they were chosen for the job! However, a confident CEO knows that they need to gain the trust of their team before they can fix anything.

Great leaders empower solutions

Despite what many managers believe about their skills and abilities, a good leader will recognise that you need to gain the confidence of your team if you want them to follow you. An ineffective leader will micromanage and control, make excessive demands and instil a sense of mistrust in their people. This is because their focus is on *output* as the key performance indicator of success; however, the best key performance indicator is actually an *outcome*.

We don't have to look far to see how a sense of ownership over an outcome can provide much more significant dedication to the work. A great leader will delegate the achievement of an outcome to their staff and trust that the multitude of tasks and outputs that are required to achieve the outcome will be delivered as part of the process.

Recall my earlier example of George being tasked with the outcome to find the needle in the haystack in chapter 3? If George had been given the clear rationale for why the needle had to be located and the timeframe required, combined with the trust that we know that he can locate it and the resources that he requires to find the needle, we give him responsibility for the outcome. George will ensure that the needle is found because we empowered him to find it without dictating 'how' it had to be completed. After all, the varying outputs are irrelevant when the outcome is achieved — George found the needle.

When you are getting to know your people as individuals, ask them about their current role (what they like and what they don't). Ask them a 'miracle' question: if they could do anything in this organisation, what would they like to do, and why? Then let them know whether you can help them achieve their vision. Once you have met with each individual, get the team together and share your vision with them. Share the challenges to achieving the vision, and then ask them how they can help you achieve these goals.

There are several psychological principles that are addressed by taking these steps with the team, which will ensure you will be afforded the support to overcome any challenges and achieve the organisation's goals. In essence, this process supports you to build rapport with each individual team member. Depending on the size of your organisation, you may not have time to meet with every individual, but you need to meet with more than half of them, and arrange to hold small group sessions with the others. As human beings, we need to connect with others to survive, these are the people who are going to help you succeed; they deserve the opportunity to learn who you are and feel understood by you.

The most fundamental error that new leadership makes is not taking time to get to know their people

The biggest mistake that most leaders make is not taking the time to get to know their people. We often see leaders going into a new team or organisation and bringing in people from their previous working life to help them solve problems. This is one of the most damaging acts by new leaders. It instils the perception that you don't trust your new team to help you, and you create a new group dynamic that usually fragments the organisation.

Most leaders will bring in people they know under the guise of 'efficiency'. However, the way that this is handled can often create much bigger problems for the culture of the organisation. If you find yourself in this position, as a new leader to an organisation and you are thinking of bringing in someone that you have worked with before, I would encourage you to take the time to reflect on the skills and abilities that person brings, and ask your people if there is anyone internally that has the required set of skills. You may be working on an inaccurate assumption. By highlighting the skills that you are seeking, if they are not already in the organisation, then your recruitment of a previous colleague doesn't create as much negative introjection. If, however, you are just wanting to bring in former colleagues because you like the way that your old team operated and you want to have that around you again, I would question why you changed roles.

You need to build camaraderie in your team because you empower them by recognising their talents or enabling them to build new skills. Failure to do this has a very negative effect on the culture. Before long, you will start to see turnover increase as people perceive that they no longer belong.

It is very difficult to mediate an organisation back together once it has become fragmented—much better to instil a sense of capability in the team you already have

---

If you truly believe that you require a specific skill set for the benefit of the organisation, then advertise the position and encourage your people to share it around. Even if the person who wins the position is someone that you have worked with previously, the perception of an open and fair process in recruitment will instil a greater sense of loyalty than any hint of nepotism will.

Great leaders are transparent.

It's not enough to simply listen to your people

One of the most effective ways of embedding psychological safety in the workplace is to ensure that concerns are dealt with as a priority. There has to be clear policies and processes, but they also have to be given a sense of value, and this is often the missing link in most Western corporate structures.

The standard approach to issues is: 'we will deal with them later, we're really busy now'. The message that is transmitted is that the person who is raising the concern isn't a priority. However, I think that we need to understand just how much effort it takes to raise a concern to a higher authority.

From a psychological perspective, when we experience a dissonance, a discomfort about a given situation, depending on our personality and our role, we will spend an awful lot of time trying to ignore the feelings before we consider taking any action. So, when a staff member comes to you with a story of discontent, they have probably felt upset by the issue for some time.

Even when they come to you reporting something that happened 'recently' (in the past 72 hours, usually), the behaviour that has tipped them over the edge is something that they have witnessed before. The fact that they are highlighting a recent issue is usually because that is a scenario in which they feel they have strong evidence of the behaviour that is the source of their concerns.

As a leader, you must take immediate action, or be perceived to be taking steps towards an action validation immediately, to avoid escalation of the issue. Try to remember that for every complaint that makes it to your office, that person will have sought validation of their perception from numerous other people in the organisation before they escalated it to you.

If you don't have the time or the interest in resolving these issues in your organisation, then you need to ensure that you have a leader whose role it is to resolve personnel conflicts. Whether that is the Chief Happiness Officer, the HR Manager, the Wizard of Wellbeing or someone else, you need to have a chief of personnel crises. That person needs to take immediate action on any concern raised by a staff member, and operate from a position of recognition validation, before proceeding to action validation.

By the time a staff member escalates an issue, they are close to breaking point

Remember: by the time the person is raising the issue to senior leadership, they are usually close to breaking point and will soon be on stress leave if they don't feel heard. This is likely to be the only opportunity that you have to mediate a resolution around the issue, and at this point there is no issue that is too small to be validated. We need to hear the concerns, validate the perception of the issue and express empathy for how they are feeling. Provide affirmation against the perceived negative behaviour, and assure the complainant that you have heard them, and that action validation will proceed. Again, reassure them that they have been heard.

It's incredible how simple the act of recognition can be:

'I'm sorry that you felt that way.'

'Yes, I can see why that must have felt awful for you.'

'What can I do to assist you with this immediately?'

These simple words have a significant impact on the wellbeing of your staff member.

Leaders who are ill prepared for this type of recognition validation process tend to jump straight into denial before taking the time to hear the concerns. Whenever you have a team member in your office raising concerns, you're usually observing someone who is extremely anxious about telling you their feelings in case they are invalidated. So, try to engage this person with your curious mind, particularly if they raise something that appears to be completely out of character for the person they are raising the issue about.

In the Western world, we have an expectation that certain situations are not going to be positive when they are out of the ordinary. When a staff member asks to speak with you privately, you are already on alert that something is up, so you're already priming your own 'fight, flight, freeze' response in your limbic system, and are already hyper-aroused. For this reason, my recommendation is to take the staff member out of the office for a walk'n'talk. Grab a coffee and make the initial conversation an informal one.

Walk'n'talk

The walk'n'talk does two things:

- It makes the meeting less 'formal'.

- It activates memory pathways in a way that helps to lower arousal.

By making the meeting less formal, the person who has raised the concern is immediately going to feel more relaxed because they are out of the office and out of earshot, and away from the prying eyes of other staff. There is nothing more anxiety provoking than feeling like you're going into the boss's office and everyone knows why you are there. Most of the time no one knows or cares, but for the person who is escalating an issue, their fear ensures that they imagine all kinds of scenarios.

By walking and talking, we are lowering anxiety; it enables the brain to access memory pathways more readily, and it also taxes the working memory. The walk'n'talk provides the brain with bilateral stimulation whilst recalling a negative event.

When we apply bilateral stimulation to a negative memory, we enable it to be appropriately processed. In this way, if the situation is one of significant concern, through telling the story, the staff member evokes emotion and is able to better rationalise the events that caused their distress. This process will clarify the concerns that are rational and valid and minimise the emotive reaction, enough so that the staff member can also better analyse their own responses.

The walk'n'talk is the most effective way to get to the bottom of problems in your organisation. It is ridiculously simple to enact, but I assure you it is one of the most powerful tools for engendering psychological safety in your business.

The walk'n'talk is one of the most powerful tools for promoting psychological safety

---

Case study: Karen

Karen was a middle-level manager in a large organisation who had recently been headhunted into a new role by a senior stakeholder in a collaboration project. Karen started the new role, and everything was flowing smoothly; her new position was closer to home and she was able to ride her motor-scooter to work. In her third week, Karen had an accident on the way to work, coming off her scooter and injuring her right side.

Although seemingly superficial, Karen suffered significant bruising and whiplash from hitting her head on the road. Karen needed to take some time off work and then was allowed to gradually return to work over several weeks.

Upon returning to the workplace, Karen noticed that her new boss seemed quite short with her and dismissive of her injuries. The supervisor themselves had a long-term health condition that resulted in chronic pain, and would often make passing comments to Karen about how she had no idea about 'real pain'. Any time that Karen needed to take time off to see a physiotherapist or doctor, the supervisor would ask questions about her physical injuries and invalidate Karen's experiences.

Although Karen was back to full-time hours within four weeks, she noticed that she was being excluded from meetings and emails related to her work. She would be called into meetings with the supervisor where she would be tasked with work that was outside of her role, but she willingly set about delivering it. However, whenever she would submit the requested work, she would be chastised in front of other staff members about the fact that what she had delivered was not what the supervisor required.

Karen understandably became confused and upset; she had never had anyone question her ability to follow directions before. She had an exemplary work record, so she struggled to find a way to resolve this communication issue. She tried to speak to the supervisor but was continuously stonewalled. She requested that the supervisor assign tasks via email to ensure that she was clear on instructions. When the supervisor refused, she started putting everything in email to her supervisor after each meeting to ensure that she was on the right track with the task, but the supervisor refused to acknowledge the email confirmation.

In frustration, Karen met with the senior manager to raise her concerns and to seek advice about resolution of the problem with her supervisor. However, it was clear that the supervisor had already advised the senior manager of her poor performance, and so Karen found herself in an even more untenable position. Once her supervisor was informed of her escalation, Karen's situation became even more isolating.

The supervisor moved Karen to an area away from the rest of the team and reallocated Karen's staff to another team leader. The fact that she had documented her work and the quality stood for itself was probably the only reason that she was not performance managed.

The worst part was — Karen couldn't understand why an 'accident' had changed the attitude of her supervisor *so* significantly! She started looking for another role in the organisation, but every time she applied for something, they would contact her supervisor for a reference.

Over this time she had learned that this was a common modus operandi for the supervisor. This person tended to have one person that they targeted. It seemed that the supervisor had been accused of bullying before and for periods of time had fulfilled roles where they had no staff. For Karen, it was nice to know that she wasn't the only one, but it wasn't helping her to move forward.

Eventually, a temporary role came up that Karen was extremely qualified for. However, she was concerned about the potential new supervisor contacting her current supervisor. Even though she was extremely stressed by the thought, she felt her only option was to speak to the new supervisor about the current situation. It was a risk because the potential new supervisor may perceive her as a troublemaker.

Karen asked for a meeting in person, just to have a general chat before she applied. At the meeting Karen gave a quick overview of her qualifications and then found an opportunity to voice her concerns to the hiring supervisor. She asked if they would please only contact previous supervisors and offered to give them contact details for all of them. Karen also noted that the position was initially only being offered as a temporary transfer for three months; she asked the supervisor to give her an opportunity to prove herself in that time and, if she wasn't satisfied, Karen would return to her current role.

Thankfully for Karen, the new supervisor gave her the opportunity to transfer. Karen was so grateful that she worked very diligently for her new supervisor, and they formed a very strong working relationship. Karen was made the second in charge in that team and eventually replaced that supervisor when they moved on.

Resolution: Karen

Unfortunately, Karen's situation is more common than you think. There are many stories of people who have suffered an injury that affected their ability to work, and who then experience bullying and harassment from their supervisor. Why would the supervisor be angry with an injured worker?

Opportunity #1: Understanding the situation from both sides

The reason that this happens is usually because the supervisor is left without a worker at short notice, there is no opportunity to backfill their position and they have no opportunity for handover — so the supervisor usually ends up having to take on the additional work. Most supervisors will take this in their stride because like most human responses, when we have empathy, we can often put ourselves in the position of the injured worker. In this way, we can quickly move past frustration and change the way we feel about the inconvenience by rationalising our situation with that of our injured worker.

Action: Ensure that you have a system of work tracking and that you regularly receive high-level updates on the work that your team leaders are progressing. Inform them that it is not about micro-managing (it really isn't), it's about supporting the progress of urgent work if there is an unexpected event.

Opportunity #2: Recognising our feelings in stressful situations

In Karen's situation, the supervisor's attitude was coloured by their own health issues. They had made a negative assessment of Karen as 'weak' because they had assessed her reports of pain against their own experience and found them wanting. The timing of this accident didn't help because Karen had not been in the role long enough to have proven her worth to the new supervisor. This is one of the reasons that we see problems arising in the first three months following a change in the workplace — we need time to prove our value. Any disruption early in the working arrangement can throw out the balance, depending upon the personalities involved.

Action: Note the tendency within yourself to become frustrated with the person that appears to be the source of stress. Try to note any frustration within yourself about the impact of that person's actions on your workload, as this is usually the impetus for retaliating by exerting your power.

Opportunity #3: Taking the time to acknowledge feelings

The supervisor was known to have taken exception towards certain people in the past, yet the senior manager chose to accept their perspective. We could spend a lot of time speculating as to why the senior manager chose to do nothing, but in the end the senior manager had formed a judgement of Karen based on the assessment of her immediate supervisor — they had an established working relationship and Karen was the unknown quantity.

Action: Ensure that if you receive an approach from a staff member outlining their circumstances, take the time to acknowledge their perspective, even if you don't agree with it — it's still their perspective and deserves to be respected and acknowledged. Just acknowledge the pain expressed by the employee and avoid all attempts to 'counter' it by expressing an opinion that is not your own.

This is why it is important that you take the time to provide recognition validation in the absence of action validation. If the senior manager had at least taken the time to empathise with Karen and agreed to make further enquiries for action validation, Karen would have felt heard. Instead, Karen's concerns were dismissed as unimportant and her feelings of being ostracised were made stronger.

The benefit of the doubt

Whenever a staff member comes to you with a problem with another one of your people, it is essential that you afford them the benefit of the doubt. All too often we choose to dismiss the issues that people raise without trying to understand the basis for them. We jump straight into action because that is how we have learned to react in the Western world.

Society in general has set up the expectation that we always have to find fault somewhere whenever there is a problem. It's the way we have come to find order in society, through rules and regulations and making judgements about a person's behaviour in consideration of those rules. Yet, many of the complexities of human beings are in the perception of their experience. When we look at the rules around bullying and harassment, or other forms of discrimination, it is the perception of the person who is feeling victimised that provides action validation of the experience under law. For most employees, the act of obtaining a legal validation of their experience is often too difficult to obtain, either due to cost or lack of mental fortitude, *not* because they couldn't meet the criteria.

As a fallback, we try to persuade our people that their perception is wrong by following some sort of assessment process, our own way of reacting to the situation. We appoint ourselves 'judge and jury' and declare a position on one side or the other. We simply don't need to follow such a process. We need to validate the individual's perception of their experience and mediate a resolution between the parties.

When I train senior managers in this process, I regularly receive comments about 'I don't have time for this!' or 'Why can't people just get on with their work!' — to which I often reply that this *is* their work.

People management is an important part of any organisation's ability to function effectively. As a leader, you need to be across any people challenges, even if you have a Chief Happiness Officer. You may delegate the mediation, but no matter what level manager you are, you will always have direct staff members who are going to raise people challenges. You can't run the business without your people, so you need to accept that your people need to feel valued and supported to operate effectively.

Why great workers aren't always great leaders

Corporate managers often rely on the assumption that the technical expert should be promoted to team leader, assuming all of the obligations for people management and not just organisational output. This is where things become problematic, especially in rigid command and control structures, like those that we see in emergency services agencies. In Australia, all emergency service agencies utilise the Australasian Inter-Service Incident Management System (AIIMS) and this informs their leadership style and structure. AIIMS provides emergency services agencies with a doctrine that enables multiple services to operate extremely effectively in stressful situations that require compliance with an order without consideration of the implications of the action. The hierarchical structure affords the surety of quick and responsive action in a highly reactive environment, like a battle zone or a fire front — but it doesn't provide training for these managers when they need to demonstrate compassion and empathy or afford a member flexibility in their work obligations.

One of the suggestions that I make to many leaders in this sector is to consider alternative management structures that take the people management out of the work delivery management. There are several reasons why this may be a good option to consider.

In technical environments, it is better to have a dedicated people manager separate to the technical delivery

---

Firstly, the ability to have a dedicated people manager who is responsible for the approval of leave and other entitlements can result in a more impartial perception about the equity of decisions. There is a common perception of bias that can develop within workplaces regarding decisions around capability in the delivery of the work. The competency of an individual to deliver work should not be tied into their access to entitlements or supports. By having a dedicated people manager, the workplace is afforded a built-in review process around recognition and performance.

You will recall the value that we place on people management in Western cultures is very low. We have somehow missed the fact that poorly managed people are unhappy and less productive than those who feel valued and empowered to perform their work to a high standard. Yet, our people are our largest resource and need to be effectively managed. Simple things go a long way towards helping an employee feel like they are part of something bigger.

If you have a dedicated people manager, they know that their role is to support the people to perform their role. They learn more about their personal situation and, due to their nature, show more empathy and understanding than a technical expert. The argument that we get from most corporates is the cost — but research shows that the best investment a company can make is in the wellbeing of its people.[26]

So how do we improve?

Part IV

Prevention and Recovery

CHAPTER 7

Industry Challenges

Known problem sectors and the quiet achievers

I regularly present at conferences that look at challenges for defence personnel, emergency services and frontline workers. As an industry group, the challenges of being exposed to difficult, and often life and death situations as part of their work naturally lends itself to traumatic experiences in the workplace. There are other elements of exposure to occupational violence that can affect police, paramedics and — perhaps surprisingly — teachers!

In addition, there are some industry sectors that are known to experience high levels of mental health challenges that go unaddressed. Not surprisingly, these are traditionally male-dominated sectors like mining and the resources sector, construction and other STEM-related industries, like information technology (IT).

I have interviewed several senior leaders for this book, including several from within these sectors, and they are often surprised to hear me say that we can prevent traumatic injuries. In defence and the emergency services sectors, there has been a belief that PTSD was just an unfortunate outcome of the job for some members. As a sector, the public safety area has started to change its language around the impact of traumatic exposure at work, but we have a long way to go from the standard 'put some cement on your cornflakes' attitudes of the past.

For the most part, these organisations are much more accepting of PTSD as a common consequence of the work. However, there is so much that can be done to improve the way that these organisations function that would reduce the occurrence of PTSD developing.

Implications of poorly managed stressors on the workforce have recently come under international scrutiny. In early 2020, two directors of a French company were found guilty of manslaughter for failing to intervene in the bullying and harassment of a staff member who ultimately took his own life. We know that the resources sector has high rates of suicide amongst its employees. How long will it be before these corporations are held to account for their failure to even attempt to improve the mental health of their workers?

Responsibility

You may recall from chapter 2 that I said that the biggest determining factor about whether a traumatic incident becomes a traumatic injury has to do with responsibility. In these industry groups, we have highly trained and specialised teams with particular skills that they must utilise under extremely stressful circumstances. For the most part, they follow routines based on scenarios that they have trained for. In many cases, they have trained their body so well that their actions follow muscle memory. They will often report that when they are in the thick of things, they are not thinking, they are responding and taking action — 'No time to think!'

Their training allows them to complete their task and achieve an outcome, and they aim for the best possible outcome: the firefighter extinguishes the fire, the police officer catches the bad guy, and the paramedic saves a life. However, when the outcome isn't the best, these people do what all humans do naturally — we go over the story in our minds, and often out loud to others, enabling us to obtain confirmation that we took the right actions and achieved the best possible outcome.

In public safety, certain circumstances will result in a higher level of arousal — when there has been a fatality or an issue involving a child, these things go against what we perceive to be 'right' in our world. These are the circumstances that will cause people to review the scenario in their mind, in their dreams and sometimes out loud. These are the situations that everyone would feel badly about, but they will affect a person more strongly if there is any similarity between the circumstances of the incident and the member's own life. In addition, the events will have a much stronger impact if the member believes that perhaps they did something wrong, or has a feeling that they could have tried something different. These two scenarios usually result in a higher level of recall of the event in our minds, but they are often not spoken about due to the shame that they invoke.

These are scenarios that we can provide pre-exposure psychoeducation about. However, these sectors are often very technical areas and the debrief that occurs is usually unpacking the situation from a purely technical perspective. In many cases, when it is identified that someone did something in the field that may have made things worse, they are openly chastised in front of others. In many of these organisations, they will also rely on sarcasm and dark humour to try and deflect the discomfort of their situation.

First responders

I interviewed several prominent leaders in the public safety sector to understand the challenges for this industry sector. The primary reason for focusing on first responders is because we know that they are at high risk for psychological injuries as a result of their work. I have spoken at many conferences that address the challenges of this sector, and I am constantly met with surprise when I say that 'we can prevent psychological injuries' — even in this sector!

I spoke with Commissioner Georgeina Whelan of the ACT Emergency Services Agency (ESA) and former Australian Defence Force; Deputy Commissioner Andrew Short of the Queensland Fire and Emergency Services (QFES); and Stuart Bartels of the Australian Institute of Police Management (AIPM) and former West Australian Police Commander.

I really wanted to try and understand the leadership challenges that this sector faces from people who have been leading these organisations for decades. The challenges that we discussed are universal to the public safety sector around the globe.

Georgeina Whelan: ACT Emergency Services Agency

When I interviewed Commissioner Georgeina Whelan of the ACT ESA, we had a very candid conversation about the difficulties of resolving the known challenges with this sector.

Georgeina had a distinguished career of over 30 years in the Australian Army before joining the ESA in November 2017 as the chief officer of the State Emergency Service (SES). Georgeina was then appointed as the commissioner of the ESA just before the Australian black summer bushfires of 2019, which then rolled into the pandemic.

Recognising the similarities between defence and emergency services roles, we discussed this sector under the banner of 'first responders' and this is a term that includes police, fire, ambulance, SES and defence. In some other areas they are referred to as public safety organisations. Georgeina believes that the similarities across these industries are all very good attributes: teamwork, leadership, coordination and the form and function around what they do. They all wear a uniform and can identify with each other, and these are really positive things.

Georgeina recognises that the sector also has its challenges, or what she prefers to see as opportunities for growth. From her perspective, organisationally, she believes that the emergency services sector is probably around ten to 15 years behind defence, as it relates to the coordination of operations. Moving from short, sharp, major operations to campaign operations.

The changing environmental landscape has resulted in the sector needing to adapt. They are now preparing for five-month fire seasons, six-month storm seasons, and the addition of challenging roles in supporting public health obligations through the pandemic. The sector around the world has had to evolve in response to global warming, in terms of its ability to manage and sustain seemingly unrelenting natural disasters.

In Australia, as a result of back-to-back years of storms, floods, bushfires and then the pandemic, Georgeina is starting to see human challenges emerge in first responders. As an industry, and as a community, she recognises that we need to continue to learn and evolve how we can better respond and care for our people.

Stigma, culture and support

Georgeina's perspective of the challenges for the emergency services sector around health and wellbeing revolve around stigma, culture and supporting volunteers. First and foremost, there is the challenge of supporting volunteers, who become 'employees' the moment they become operational. Due to their work being voluntary, they often don't realise they can come forward and report the health and wellbeing challenges that may develop because of their service.

Culturally, the emergency services community, whether full time or part time, are tough. They are happy to report falling off a building, falling down a ladder or a broken ankle, but are still far less likely to report any sense of emotional struggle, psychological trauma or mental health concern. For this sector there remains significant stigma around psychological wellbeing. Georgeina believes this is an education issue. These are barriers to accessing care. By not coming forward, members remain unaware of what support is available to them.

Like many leaders in this field, Georgeina believes that there is a whole body of work that needs to be developed about how to change these challenges, but as I explained to her: the work has already been done, it just hasn't been adopted across the sector in a comprehensive way.

Georgeina believes that the sector is only really starting to have these conversations post the 2019–20 bushfire season, and then only because they are confronted with statistics that say their people are hurting after the reality of fighting bushfires for five months, and seeing the devastation, the loss of lives, loss of property, loss of livestock and loss of community.

Georgeina recalled a conversation with a rural firefighter who had returned from fighting bushfires in northern New South Wales (NSW). He had been a member of the rural fire service for 15 years, and had regularly put his hand up for training and deployment interstate. He recalled a moment when the black summer fires crossed the Queensland border into NSW. He said it felt different and it really hit him hard this time — the sense of loss. They are used to going in for two or three days, working really hard, then it's done. They celebrate the wins when they save a property, and they commiserate with the community when they lose a property. However, the unrelenting force of the black summer fires was different. These communities had already been devastated by fires and floods. They had just got back on their feet and now their community had been destroyed again. The loss was overwhelming. The death and destruction, and the loss of livestock, flora and fauna — they had nothing left. The firefighter brought that sense of true loss home with him. He felt like he couldn't help them as much as he would normally.

What we are now seeing is the impact of that loss on our first responders, but also on their families, their children and the community as a whole. This seems to have altered the landscape of emergency services in Australia. Georgeina notes:

More people are coming forward and sharing these challenges, and we are becoming more aware of it. Now we're starting to talk about it, but what are we actually going to do to resolve it?

Andrew Short: Queensland Fire and Emergency Services

I interviewed Assistant Commissioner Andrew Short of the QFES, and we had a very open conversation at a time when Andrew was juggling the impact of the second major flood threat in Queensland in 2022.

Andrew joined the Queensland Fire Service as a firefighter back in 1986, and was appointed as an Assistant Commissioner in QFES in 2016. Similar to the ACT ESA, QFES is a construct of a number of emergency services comprising about 45 000 members, including 35 000 volunteers. It's a significant community workforce.

Andrew and I have spoken on earlier occasions about the challenges for the sector with regards to the known risk for members to develop PTSD. However, we had also spoken about a report that was published by Beyond Blue[27] in which members of emergency services organisations had indicated that the chance of developing PTSD was just as likely from a poor workplace culture, due to bullying and harassment, as it was from any other traumatic exposure in the field.

Through his own journey, Andrew identified his own experience of interacting with both staff and volunteers over a number of years, and he developed a pretty clear idea of the impact of a dysfunctional workplace. When the Beyond Blue report came out, he was not actually surprised by the statement. The fact that the impact of organisational culture is as great as the impact that comes from operational work really shocked leaders in the frontline sector who probably didn't see that coming. For Andrew, it indicated that the effort they are investing in trying to improve the workplace environment, and all the challenges that go with that, are justified.

It is quite challenging to improve workplace culture across a large organisation, but especially challenging when you cover a large geographic area, and most of those areas are managed by a network of volunteers. This means that QFES relies on the local teams to be self-sufficient to a large extent. If a critical incident occurs that has a high cost on the individuals in terms of psychological stimulus, they rely on remote teams to take the first initial steps to encourage dialogue with the affected member.

Andrew has become more aware of research that highlights the importance of the first 24 hours post-incident. As a result, QFES has become more active in debriefing as a form of engagement. This means facilitating a safe environment where members can just talk. However, he recognises that one of the perceived norms of the sector is that you do this work, and it's tough sometimes, yet you are just expected to knuckle down, tough it out and see it through — 'Put some cement on your weeties!' The industry as a whole is making efforts to be more proactive in this area, and they are doing a lot better than they were, but it really does rely on the local leadership to do the right thing.

QFES do have a critical incident categorisation system in place, so particular incident categories have specific flags. If there's a deceased person involved or if it's a particularly complex and difficult rescue or something with strong people aspects and emotion to it, they have strong triggers for activating support. They have a strong peer-support network, which they have invested in over a long time, but there are some other triggers that indicate that they need to do more than just provide peer support.

Andrew believes that they need to have someone qualified with psychological experience to be on site for that team. In serious incidents, they provide extra support by having a couple of counsellors from the central support services team present, but Andrew is aware that it can be an area fraught with danger when people feel like they are being pushed into disclosing how they feel. It's a sensitive area; a real juggling act.

Balancing leadership

Andrew recognises the challenges of achieving balanced leadership in the sector. He is aware that the recruitment mechanisms within the sector probably put technical specialists into leadership positions, knowing that they're incredibly strong in the field, but they may have some gaps in people skills. The marketplace is currently not providing any other solutions, so as a result, the sector is forced to compromise a little.

Andrew believes that it is possible to improve people skills. If a person is committed to improving self-awareness, then by extension social awareness and self-regulation, then everyone can shift their thinking. For some it is only a very small shift in thinking, some really thrive in leadership roles, but there may be some people who will not be able to take on certain leadership attributes or capabilities.

AIIMS is the management approach utilised by emergency services, military and policing, albeit in different ways. It takes a functional approach to the management of critical incidents to ensure there is someone in charge of operations, another in charge of planning, and others in logistics and information communication. Andrew is aware that emergency services are stepping away from a purely operational and incident grounds focus. Most organisations have HR practitioners in place, but they are not yet integrated into the operational teams. That speaks to how senior leadership in the sector values the contribution of people specialists and the value they can bring. Andrew acknowledges that it is definitely a work in progress.

Andrew is aware that there is a lot of research indicating that a person's individual experience in the workplace is strongly associated with who they are working for. Whoever their boss is will determine what sort of workplace experience they have when tough times come. It's hard when you have high-end, critical incident people with young families who are always under pressure. As a father, he is aware that when the phone rings to say a child is sick, or there has been an accident, that means the team member has to leave the workplace pretty quickly to be able to deal with that.

Andrew has seen many examples where the leader has been incredibly respectful and supportive to that person, saying, 'Absolutely, that's important. Off you go. What are you dealing with? We'll look after it!' He has also seen examples in which that person leaves work, but feels like they've let the team down because of the way the communication has occurred when they've shared their obligations to their family with their boss.

It's the recognition of the shift of pressure or stress. If that boss is under duress and was looking for something to be done that day, they can certainly make their disappointment known, even if it's not in words. A compassionate leader can acknowledge the impact on their workload or mission, but don't present that as being the priority, because the most important thing in that moment is that member being able to deal with something that is creating personal distress.

The experience you have when you're not available to your workplace, whether it's because of a sick child or a serious health event, the person that you work for, they're the focal point. Even if that leader reaches out to a HR specialist for advice on what they need to do in terms of process, their reaction to the immediate need of their staff member as a human being will be front of mind for the worker. In the end people don't remember what happened, they remember how they felt or how they were treated. That is the notion that resonates for Andrew as it really speaks to humans being a 'chemical cocktail' of emotion. As much as there are some people in large organisations who see people as a distraction from the work, the work can't be done without the people.

Teaching mental health

To support increased mental health literacy, QFES has provided education in mental health first aid. They are trying to improve the psychological response to individuals or issues that happen in people's personal lives that may impact their work. Realistically, we can't expect our leaders to be all things to all people, and leaders are going to have clear boundaries and expectations on what they can or should do. Certainly, one of the things QFES reinforce is to not try to work it all out yourself and think that you need to have all the answers.

In recent times, in line with a lot of government focus, QFES focused on the impact of domestic violence on their members, as they know that what transpires between the affected member and their leadership connection to the organisation will directly determine how supported that person feels. When a member has a lot going on, the last thing they want is their workplace complicating things for them.

Andrew believes the same approach applies for all psychological challenges, but recognises that the sector still finds interpersonal difficulties challenging to support. There is a strong need for increased mental health literacy and exposure to managing these challenges for staff across the sector.

Andrew is aware that knowledge of psychological distress increased over the pandemic, and psychological wellbeing and best practice is discussed within the sector more than ever. He believes that there are more opportunities to learn, and an increased number of resources that people can access. However, he is also aware that doesn't mean that the right people are accessing the right resource or doing the right thing all the time.

The sector may need more resources to be able to do it better, but sometimes that is just an excuse. There isn't an organisation that doesn't operate in a resource-constrained environment. On the whole, Andrew believes that their frontline leaders are doing the right thing, the majority of the time, in terms of their interaction with the people in their teams who are having problems. The better the leader, the less fallout. Once people start to engage with the workers compensation system, things can go a little off track (I unpack this challenge further in chapter 8). The better our leaders become at something, the more they understand the problem or challenge, the more they see the complexity. Andrew says, 'The more we know, the more we realise what we don't know.'

Frontline leaders are doing their best, but interpersonal difficulties can be challenging to support

---

I asked Andrew about his own experience of psychological distress in the workplace. He said that he absolutely experienced challenges, and in his early working life there were some occasions where he didn't handle it well. He recognises that the earlier version of himself had some hard lessons to learn, and needed to build the self-awareness and self-honesty to acknowledge the challenges. Andrew says that he is no different to anyone else, rationalising or justifying his actions, or using other methods to distract himself or lighten the load. Like many people in these sectors, he looked forward to a drink at the end of the shift, until he realised that it's actually a form of self-medication that many people struggle with. Andrew says that as a young man he couldn't see that, but now he recognises the feeling. When he feels like he 'needs' a drink, he now questions himself as to what that is about.

Andrew tries to stick to the rule, 'if you want to drink, drink to dream to be happier, but don't drink to be happy'. He's not against enjoying a wine on occasion, but really understanding why you're having it has been an important step. He recognises that he won't get it right all the time; he recognises that he can't achieve perfection.

It's the recognition of the distress build-up, even though those moments are probably less common in more senior roles, although by their nature, senior leadership roles can be stressful. Andrew believes that we need to have tools and approaches to help ourselves through. You also don't need to cope with it all yourself: Andrew recognises the need to debrief, and he maintains a network around him that can support him. Not because someone can fix his problems for him, but his support network helps him unpack the challenges, because they help him reflect. Andrew sees the self-awareness to be honest with yourself as an incredibly important skill to develop.

Stuart Bartels: Australian Institute of Police Management

I met Stuart Bartels several times prior to my formal interview, as the AIPM had been looking into the challenges of mental health in the public safety sector and how it might support the senior leaders who engage in their senior leadership program.

Stuart spent 36 years in the Western Australia Police, finishing there as a commander. His career crossed a diverse range of portfolios, and he spent a lot of time in rural Western Australia in frontline policing. Stuart was the officer in charge of several police stations over many years. He spent over a decade in various areas of forensics, and then started a senior executive career. At this stage of a policing career, there is no longer any specificity as to where you work or what you're doing; the role changes into a more executive role.

Forensics is a tough gig in policing. It's just the nature of the work. Stuart dealt with homicides, sudden deaths, rapes, violent crimes and the aftermath of those. He spent a lot of time at the mortuary, and recognises the challenges of being exposed to these types of unnatural events.

I'm very aware of the impact that this type of regular exposure has on most people, and I asked Stuart if he struggled. He doesn't believe that the work itself affected him like it has others, and he pondered whether it would have been more helpful if it had. Stuart agreed that there are things that he saw that he would prefer to unsee, and that there were events in his career where he was under the microscope, in which he did question his judgement, wondering if he made a mistake. Stuart believes that his resilience came from the fact that he had a good life and a great support system: he has a good marriage, their kids are healthy and life is good. Because of this, he believes that the reality of his forensic career never affected him too greatly. Stuart acknowledges that he was always able to compartmentalise his work and home life pretty well.

Stuart's experience isn't an isolated one. Exposure to traumatising situations alone is not responsible for traumatic injuries. When we consider how occupational traumatic exposure impacts people, even in frontline work environments or emergency service work, people don't automatically develop traumatic injuries from exposure. The key to developing a traumatic injury lies in a sense of responsibility or lack of safety or control. Particularly in policing, the scenes they attend and the things they are exposed to are not usually situations that they feel responsible for. The development of a traumatic injury is dependent on the attribution of responsibility. If there was an engagement that the member was blaming themselves for, for what they did or didn't do on a scene, this is more likely to result in an injury. This is where the importance of good leadership can be vital in managing the debrief.

This is where Stuart's passion for leadership has really driven his work with the AIPM. The AIPM has partnered with Griffith University to research 'Leadership for Wellness' in public safety organisations. They want to better understand the role of the organisation, organisational justice and specific leaders themselves, in the wellness of members in frontline working environments. What is becoming really clear is that the leadership approach often stands between the experience of trauma and the outcome for the member. This research has revealed that there is often a 'black box' between these two elements. The notion is that the 'black box' represents an extraneous variable, a 'something else' that is going on for the member — be that an organisational justice issue, specific leader/ follower interaction, marital breakdown, health issues or some other challenge beyond the traumatic experience alone. The AIPM are hoping that this understanding opens the door for a leadership-led preventative approach — essential when leading for wellness.

Wellness culture

I directed Stuart to the Beyond Blue Report[27] that found that poor workplace culture can cause as many problems in terms of traumatic injuries, as exposure to traumatic experiences in the field for frontline workers in emergency service organisations. Stuart agreed that culture is complex. He is seeing that emergency services are really leaning into wellness at a whole organisational level, from policies and practices through to legislation and programs. Stuart sees that culture is far more complex than policies and programs, and he believes that hands on, direct leadership plays a huge role in culture. He is curious to understand what that culture is and where it comes from? What drives it? How does it link to poor mental health outcomes?

From my perspective, I see that a lot of the impact on poor cultural development in public safety organisations can be explained by the ongoing exposure to threatening and traumatic situations that has traditionally relied on a tough attitude to diminish the impact. We hear a lot in these sectors about the need to be strong, and that the expression of emotion is often met with deflection and black humour, backed up by alcohol to numb themselves and avoid the reality of their experiences. The denial of emotion tends to lead to aggression in many areas of life: some will go to the gym, others will fight with their spouse. More need to be educated to recognise the signs and be afforded better solutions. Perhaps then, culture will improve.

The repression of emotion produces anger to contain it — anger that's misdirected onto unrelated areas of life

---

I highlighted to Stuart that many organisations have mental health strategies or wellbeing programs in place, but that they are often great motherhood statements that don't translate into action on the ground. Most have little specificity in measurable outcomes and often there is not an internal 'champion' appointed who is responsible for the delivery. Stuart agrees that this is how it has been done in the past, but he firmly believes that the sector is really striving to improve outcomes for their people. There is also new legislation proposed in Australia that will potentially hold leaders to account for the negative mental health outcomes of their people.

Legislation is important in helping to change attitudes, but as we have seen in many other areas of workers compensation, having a legal framework to hold people accountable is only as effective as the enforcement of it. If the injured worker has to engage in a battle to have the legislation enforced, then the outcome for the individual is far worse than if the legislative framework didn't exist. More on this in chapter 8.

Stigma

We must change how a disclosure around mental health challenges affects career progression. Certainly, in defence circles, reporting a psychological challenge potentially means the end of your career. The frontline services sector has to recognise that mental health is something that we all deal with, and that we all experience challenges at different points. It shouldn't be a career-ending disclosure, rather it should be the opportunity for the employer to be able to provide support.

There are far too many examples of people disclosing their difficulties to their leaders, only to find themselves being removed from operational duty. As a result, we find that many members will fail to report their challenges for fear of being 'stood down', and this removes them from the sense of camaraderie that may provide them with the impetus to recover.

We also don't provide this sector with much education about the impact of traumatic experiences on our brain over time. The sector is full of examples of numbing avoidance to the impacts — for example, the police who head to the pub straight after work for a few beers. The tendency towards 'black humour' in these sectors is very strong — these are human responses to help our brains deal with the difficult reality of what we are seeing and experiencing.

As an industry sector, emergency services can support their members to recover. They can find injured members alternative employment, but they need to have the systems and programs in place to enable this in a supportive way.

This sector needs to be educated about a system of healthcare, a system of response, and a commitment to recovery. Without the certainty of process and impact, then what we have is the unknown and that creates fear. That fear reinforces the stigma and stops people declaring that they are unwell and need assistance.

The resources sector

The resources sector has maintained a vigilant focus on physical workplace health and safety. Historically, efforts were directed toward the identification and mitigation of safety risk, and the promotion of workplace culture that aims to protect the physical welfare of the individual and their workmates. Over the past few years, there has been a widening of this focus to include the wellbeing and mental health of those working in these industries. There is now a strong body of evidence that attention to mental health can bring substantial benefits to an industry. This approach has been supported in principle by the Minerals Council of Australia in their 2015 'Blueprint for Mental Health and Wellbeing'.

The main concern with the approach outlined in this blueprint is that there are a number of areas that have been identified as 'possible actions that the minerals industry, companies, sites or employees may undertake'. However, in the past eight years there has been little change in the mental health and wellbeing of workers in the resources sector. The main reason for this is that, in order to achieve a goal, research shows that you have to ensure that certain criteria are met. The blueprint provided several ideas around improving mental health, but didn't get into the specifics around ownership for these ideas or the what, where, when, how, who and why. Without specific outcomes that are measurable, and without holding someone to account for them, the chances of success pale into insignificance.

In order to achieve real and lasting cultural change for the sector, there must be specific elements that are clearly identified and guidance provided about exactly what activities are going to result in improved mental health and wellbeing for the cohort. They need to have timeframes for achievement and a plan for getting there. Then the outcomes need to be measured and monitored for ongoing and iterative improvement.

It's not all about stigma...

There is a strong belief in these male-dominated sectors that these problems exist due to stigma. Although it may be true that there is a significant level of stigma across these industry sectors, it does not have to be a barrier to help-seeking. In fact, I published research in 2018 about increasing help-seeking intention.[28] We can increase help-seeking intention, especially in men, but they need to be hearing the right message.

Lack of focus

Data on mental health needs within the resources sector is limited. Research in affiliated sectors has been more robust, and some of the outcomes can be extrapolated due to their correlation.

Prior to the pandemic, one in five Australians reported a mental illness each year, for miners it is one in three. That means that there are over 93 000 resources workers, predominantly men, who are likely experiencing a mental health issue at any given time. There are several reasons for this, including higher than average levels of ex-services personnel working in the sector, remote working conditions in fly in, fly out (FIFO) and drive in, drive out (DIDO) roles, and anecdotal evidence around substance use. It's important to note that, since the pandemic, four in five Australians report some level of psychological distress. The mental health impacts are not only on the worker, but can influence the mental health of their families. In Australia, the sector employs 2 per cent of the population but influences over 9 per cent of the population.

Conservative estimates of cost to the industry, including from lowered productivity, are between A$320 million and A$450 million per year, or around $300 000 to $400 000 annually for an average site. However, these numbers were based on the impact of only 10 000 affected employees. The real number is almost 10-fold.

Marion's story

Marion and her husband John were encouraged by a friend to apply to work in the mining sector as dump truck drivers. Their friend was aware of a remote mine that had commenced a new initiative to recruit couples to train as drivers, to encourage diversity but also to support the management of shift work, and try and keep workers in the remote mining community, rather than having the higher turnover of FIFO workers. There were good financial incentives, and so both Marion and John applied and were offered employment.

From early in the training program, Marion was given instruction, the same as her husband. However, as the training process progressed, John was put into a truck on his own whereas Marion was kept in a 'jockey' position for months on end — essentially sitting in the cab with another driver to 'observe' their driving process. When Marion pushed for opportunities to access the additional training to progress her to the next level, she was often paired with a trainer who was overtly hostile and she became quite nervous. Two senior staff seemed to have a personality clash with Marion, for reasons unknown. Regardless, it appeared that they didn't want Marion to receive the training she required. Without the training, she would be unable to meet her obligations under her employment contract to be working completely independently within six months.

Marion was experiencing systematic harassment and intimidation from the trainers, which undermined her confidence. In addition, the crew supervisor and leading hand, who would provide radio instructions about where to pick up a load and where to dump it, would often berate her on the radio for doing things wrong.

On one occasion, the supervisor gave Marion instructions that were in breach of company policy. When she queried the instructions, which she knew were a breach, she was repeatedly told to just do as she was instructed. When she tried to confirm that this is what was being requested of her, she was meet with silence on the two-way radio. Marion felt so pressured that she did as she was instructed, knowing it was a breach for which she could be terminated. As expected, she was reprimanded for breaching procedure, even though it was the supervisor who instructed her to perform the breach. As punishment, Marion was stood down for the remainder of the shift. A couple of her fellow crew members let her know that the team leaders were all standing around the two-way radio and could hear her asking for clarification, yet they ignored her request.

There were a couple of supportive team members who tried to assist her, including one of the most senior driving instructors. This particular instructor told her that she actually drove better than her husband. When they returned to base at the end of the shift, that instructor attempted to get Marion 'signed off' but the superintendent refused to agree to it. There was an argument between the two men, and Marion never knew the outcome, but she wasn't rostered with that instructor again.

Marion experienced extreme harassment and intimidation in the workplace in a clear attempt to get her to quit. Marion had a very strong personality: she was tenacious and committed to stick at it and overcome the challenges, to show them that she was capable of doing the job. However, the constant belittling, undermining and overt harassment and intimidation that she experienced every shift had really started to take its toll on Marion. She was really struggling to push herself to turn up to work every day.

About five months into her employment, Marion was on shift when she had a particularly nasty interaction with one radio operator. Due to the constant stress she felt in the workplace, Marion had a near miss with another truck. She was instructed to come back to base and make a report. Instead of making a report she was instructed to go into the office where she was verbally abused by her crew supervisor who physically stood over her and berated her. Conveniently, there were no witnesses. Marion was then instructed to go for a drug and alcohol test, which, although it is standard procedure, pushed Marion too far. In her anger, she quit on the spot.

In the hours after Marion quit, she started to spiral about why she couldn't get things right. She had started to question and berate herself constantly, and this was overlaid with a constant niggling question of 'why'? Why did they target her more than some of the other women? Was it just her strong personality? Or did they have some other reason to target her?

Just 36 hours after she quit, Marion suffered a stress-induced stroke. The prolonged exposure to extreme stress was too much for her brain to cope with. It took several months for Marion to get an accurate diagnosis, and she has gone through years of recovery since. She is still unable to work, and extremely stressful situations will lead to a full palsy on her left side, still to this day, almost ten years later.

Marion's claim under workers compensation was denied because she had 'quit'. Like many other workers compensation claims for harassment, the supervisors claimed her issues were based on poor performance and her claim was denied because it was deemed as 'reasonable management actions executed reasonably'. As a result of this denial, Marion's mental health deteriorated even further. She kept berating herself for being impulsive, rather than taking herself off to the doctor for some support for her stress. If she had done the latter, she may have received compensation. As such, the feeling of persecution compounded and had a significant impact on her long-term mental health.

Thankfully, John was an incredibly supportive husband and Marion was still the same person underneath the trauma: strong and tenacious. Marion took herself off to therapy, driving several hundred kilometres each way to engage in Eye Movement Desensitisation and Reprocessing (EMDR) Therapy, trauma therapy that she says saved her life. It took several years, but eventually, Marion was able to walk and talk again, she was left with a stutter, but she has been able to recover for the most part.

Management as power

In my experience with the resources sector, and other known problem sectors like emergency services and construction, the challenge is that there is a level of control given to middle managers that enables them to feel that they hold power over the people in their workplace. Many people in these positions wield power over new starters, and ensure that the team that they lead is made up of people who they like and feel they can control. The structure of the organisation enables this level of power because the responsibility for the HR administration is often reduced to the level of site or shift operation.

Very few large companies in these sectors examine the aggregate data of their staff retention, turnover or leave, independent of the site management. The lack of transparency into the daily workings of any site results in an ability for management to wield significant influence over the culture of each site. When it comes time for the annual report, the organisation's aggregated data is collated to provide an overall picture of the company as a whole, and sometimes high-level data is reported for the whole organisation, skimming over the top of any particular site. Very rarely do these organisations have a traffic light system set up to assist them to identify personnel 'hotspots'.

One of the things that I do with organisations is support them to set up a traffic light system that will give more senior leadership insight into the hotspots. This is how we can look into challenging cultural pockets within larger organisations — there is a lot in our management data that we don't cross-reference to identify causal attributions. We need to start doing this as it enables the C-Suite to see where there may be a potential spot fire starting to burn in the organisation, and enable you to implement some mitigation strategies before it turns into a bushfire.

Women as minority groups

We don't have to look far to see that many of the known sectors where psychological injuries develop are often male-dominated cultures. It is not only women who report psychosocial injuries in these sectors, although the ratio is higher for women for workers compensation claims. The other statistic that can't be denied is that the rates of suicide in male members of these sectors are a lot higher than the national average for other industry types.

The retention rates for women in most of the known problem sectors are lower than for men. There is a diversity opportunity that needs to be considered here for a variety of reasons, including prolific research that demonstrates the benefits of diversity on financial and operating performance across all sectors.

The proportion of female workers in mining is one of the lowest across all economic sectors, comprising between 5 and 10 per cent of the global workforce.[29] Extractive industries have historically been male dominated, and there has been little change to female participation rates in comparison to other industry sectors. There is not just an under-representation at the coalface: mining is the worst-performing industry in the world in terms of inclusion of women in C-Suite and board positions, closely followed by oil and gas. Efforts must be made to foster the promotion of women into senior leadership positions.[29]

To be fair, the women's liberation movement in mining experienced a 30-year lag behind other industries. Across the world, women were prevented from working in underground mining by a 1935 decision by the International Labour Organization (ILO). However, many countries that initially ratified the convention have since denounced it, including Australia (1988), Canada (1978), Chile (1997) and South Africa (1996). These countries are now largely signatories to the ILO's Convention 176, which covers the rights of all workers.[30]

Despite the reversal of representation under law, the growth of female workers in mining and other resource sectors has been slow, as it is in other traditionally male-dominated industries like defence, fire, police and ambulance. The slow wheels of change have progressed faster in some developed countries, however, the cultural change required to ensure that women are fully embraced and engaged in equal roles in the public safety sector has been a product of some positive discrimination strategies. Unfortunately, positive discrimination in recruitment takes much longer to permeate into the overall organisational culture.

Why does gender representation have an impact on psychosocial safety?

Despite the increasing number of women in leadership roles, women experience unique challenges in leadership positions. Traditionally these challenges have been attributed to key biological differences between genders, such as differences in confidence, risk-taking tendencies and leadership style. Unsurprisingly, this assessment has disadvantaged the perception of women leaders generally.[31, 32]

Confidence

This is challenging for women who may struggle to believe in their own abilities and experience, but also need to exert great effort to communicate confidence in their leadership style. Body language (i.e., lowered eye contact and hunched shoulders), qualifying statements (i.e., 'I think' or 'I'm wondering') and apologetic language (i.e., 'I'm sorry to bother you') can influence the perception of a woman's leadership capability.[33] This, in turn, leads to assumptions about female leaders and their emotional expression, risk-taking and decision-making, culminating in the perception that female leaders are 'softer' than their male counterparts.

Add to this the reality that a woman's confidence can be affected by their social comparison to men. It has been suggested that women question their competence when compared to their male counterparts, even though many of those women have traditionally commanded a stronger position in leadership in organisational hierarchies.[33]

Despite some evidence that confidence differences exist between genders in leadership, other neuroscience work suggests that these differences are simply mistaken for self-awareness or situational realities. Research shows that men report higher feelings of confidence before or during decision-making processes, however, these differences between men and women shrink when we assess their confidence after a decision has been made. Women tend to feel more confident beforehand when they have information to support such a claim (i.e., previous experience of success). Perhaps the bravado of the male species is mistaken for true confidence.

Risk

There is a general perception that women exhibit less risk-taking behaviour because they apply a stronger emotional perspective to their risk assessment, and differences in emotion lead to differences in risk behaviour. When confronted with uncertainty, a common leadership experience due to the ever-changing nature of business, women are more likely to respond with fear, and men are more likely to respond with anger.[32] Both fear and anger have unique impacts on risk perception. Both emotions activate our amygdala into a 'fight, flight, freeze' response. Anger, as our 'fight' response, will increase the motivation to act, particularly in a risky way. By contrast, fear, as our 'flight/freeze' response, will diminish the motivation to engage in risk-taking.[32]

Neuroscientific evidence confirms these key gender differences are controlled by the limbic system, which contains the subcortical areas: amygdala (emotional reactivity), hippocampus (memory formation), septal nuclei (pleasure seeking) and nucleus accumbens (reward centre); and the orbitofrontal cortex (decision-making). The limbic system plays a key role in individual processing of risk,[33] and as humans, our emotional experiences of life are largely controlled by the limbic system. A risky situation activates different areas of this system for women and men. Women activate multiple areas in the limbic system, leading them to pause and feel, rather than jump into action. Whereas in men, the amygdala activates them into a fight response, leading men to engage in risky behaviour.

Leadership style

When considering leadership style, we typically focus on how leaders behave and their effectiveness in the eyes of their people. The most common typological difference between leaders is whether they are more task oriented — associated with transactional leadership, or relationship oriented — associated with transformational leadership.

Regarding gender differences in style, women tend to lead in a more transformational style, whereas men tend to focus on transactional leadership and exhibit both the rewards and punishment elements of this style. The relational focus of women is evidenced by their democratic and participatory behaviours, and their tendency to make decisions based on intuition and emotion. This is in stark contrast to men who tend to lead more autocratically, with decisiveness and a sense of reciprocity.[31]

Emotional intelligence is important in leadership. Emotions play a key role in facilitating social connection, and the ability to understand the emotions of others is essential to compassionate leadership. Leaders achieve connection with their people by demonstrating effective regulation and expression of emotion, and through empathy. These two capabilities work hand in hand to navigate most social interactions, including leadership.

Effective emotional regulation and expression, combined with empathy are key to compassionate leadership

---

There is a growing body of research that shows that women leaders are better at managing the needs of their people. Research on leadership style suggests that women are indeed more empathic, intuitive and sensitive to the needs of others, and this is backed up by neuroscience. Women are more perceptive to their environments, and are more likely to be affected by context, meaning they have exceptional skill in navigating social situations and adapting their behaviour accordingly. In contrast, men may 'stick to the plan' despite contextual cues. This difference can be explained by inherent biological differences in the brain.[33]

We know that our brain's mirror neurons are strongly involved in social cognition, including empathy. The expression of emotion is strongly indicated in our faces through a variety of micro-muscle movements. From the time we are babies, we learn to respond to facial expression to regulate emotion, and this is done through the activation of our mirror neurons. Mirror neurons work much like seeing ourselves in a mirror. When we experience an emotion such as sadness, this emotion shows on our face. When others see our face, their mirror neurons are activated, and their face mimics the same expression, enabling us to actually feel the pain of the other person (empathy).

This is such a strong phenomenon involved in the formation of social bonds that I provide training to leaders and therapists that I supervise around the use of Botox. You may wonder what on earth a personal cosmetic enhancement has to do with leadership or empathy, but it's actually a reasonably new, yet critical, consideration in the perception of our leadership. You see, Botox means that our mirror neurons can't activate, thereby reducing empathy activation. This is not only a consideration for you as a leader, but also a consideration when you are faced with a conflict between team members. Long-term Botox use has been shown to reduce the expression of empathy, due to the inhibition of our normal facial muscle movement. I'm not saying that you shouldn't use it, but we need to be aware of the long-term impacts on our normal empathy triggers if we choose to use it.

The ability to empathise with the perspective of others is essential to key models of leadership, such as transformational leadership, demonstrated understanding of the experiences and needs of people. Women may indeed be more empathic and, therefore, more relational leaders than men.[31]

Despite the neuroscience, I believe that men are able to learn to become more transformational leaders. In fact, I believe that the pandemic has given rise to a significant improvement in compassionate leadership. I am often approached by the CEO or board chairperson of a large organisation to support them in improving workplace culture and the wellbeing of their people, and they are often men. They will admit that they understand the obligation to support people, but don't necessarily feel the empathy or have the patience to address the expression of emotion in the workplace. When I ask about the makeup of the C-suite of these organisations, they are unsurprisingly male dominant.

I'm really not trying to say that men aren't capable of compassionate leadership, I'm saying that it comes more naturally to women. What we need to learn is to respect the emotional intelligence of women, and seek to gain insights from their natural abilities.

I am also saying that the known problem sectors all demonstrate a significant scarcity of women in the workforce, but particularly in senior leadership roles. The resources industry, public safety organisations and the STEM sector in general are all sectors with a low representation of women. In addition, they often have poor workplace culture and gender acceptance challenges that result in high attrition rates for women entering the sector. If we are going to change this, we need a clear plan and some accountability for the outcomes.

TechDiversity

I spoke to Luli Adeyemo, Managing Director of TechDiversity and founder of the technology marketing agency Best Case Scenario. I had been introduced by a mutual connection because TechDiversity have taken a strong stand on trying to make a big difference in the way the STEM Industry approaches their people and culture.

TechDiversity is an industry alliance committed to amplifying diversity awareness and achieving a culture of inclusion through conversation, collaboration and action. It has the support of industry groups and businesses, in addition to the Victorian Government. Its #TechDiversity Awards showcases what can be achieved across sectors in building diversity and inclusion. It has a focus on strengthening frameworks to increase the participation of all diverse groups within a technology workforce, including:

- Cultural diversity

- Racial diversity

- Religious diversity

- Age diversity

- Sex / Gender diversity

- Sexual orientation

- Disability

Luli has over 30 years of experience curating content for thought leadership discussions and campaigns within the technology, Government, FinTech and health sectors. Prior to running her company Best Case Scenario, Luli worked for Gartner heading up their Asia/Pacific conference business. Luli's unique professional network has seen her involved in initiatives that propel innovation and business growth.

Luli and her team continue to work with clients in curating thought leadership content and delivering it effectively to enrich their client's customer experiences. Current and past clients include: Microsoft, Intel, AIIA, Newfound Global, HP, ASUS, Dataminr, InfoMedix and more. Luli is very experienced across the technology sector and it was her love of the industry, combined with her frustration with its notable lack of diversity in the sector that led her in early 2020 to join TechDiversity, a not for profit alliance established in 2015.

Luli highlights that the technology sector has it's roots firmly in middle class masculinity not fertile ground for embracing diversity. The image of the white, male tech geek making big with a computer and an internet connection is still ubiquitous when we think of the big players in the tech industry — the portrayal outlined in the 2016 movie *Hidden Figures* provides a classic insight into the foundations of the industry. This is why Luli and her fellow leaders at TechDiversity believe that it is so important to look at the industry as it stands, to see where this stereotype is being challenged and, if not, why not.

Over the course of the pandemic there's been a significant increase in the focus on diversity in tech, with reporting indicating that minorities represent less than 20 per cent of major companies such as Google[34]. Google made Diversity a specific focus in 2022 and their published highlights show that they are making progress with 2022 being their best year for hiring women globally (37.5 per cent) and in their Black+ and Latinx+ hires in the US growing faster than their global community overall. In a focus on leadership, Google improved Black+, Latinx+ and Native American+ leadership representation by 27 per cent and women by 9 per cent[35]. This indicates that a focus on strategies and programs designed to change culture can be very effective — but they need to become a priority.

There has been a focus on improving the number of women in tech, but these drivers and initiatives have largely lacked intersectionality, leading to improvements in gender diversity, but little improvement when it comes to other diversity attributes such as cultural heritage, worldview, language, or non-binary identification or neurodiversity — a common attribute in the tech sector.

The issue is not limited only to large corporates — a 2019 report into women in technology[36] found that only half of all start-ups have women on their leadership team.

It's important to recognise that organisational culture change needs senior leadership representation and focus to ensure that things happen. Google appointed their Chief Diversity Officer five years ago, but it has only been in the last 12 months that the numbers are starting to reflect their expanded focus on diversity — no doubt fuelled by some of the changes to the way we work that have been brought about by the pandemic. Cultural change is a 'long game'.

Luli notes that inclusive organisations do not view diversity as just policy, but acknowledge the core value it can bring to organisations – diversity for the sake of diversity doesn't work. Luli wants to eliminate any notion that inclusivity and diversity is just a tick on an organisation's corporate social responsibility policy, and show that diversity and inclusion add significant value to any business.

Luli's passion for diversity, equity and inclusion comes from personal experience. A female owner of her own strategic events and marketing company, she is black and has a visual impairment — she ticks all the boxes for inclusivity and diversity. Not one to focus on the negativity surrounding discrimination, Luli admits that like many before her, she has been subjected to harassment and discrimination in her past. This is a big part of her personal drive for improving the sector for others.

TechDiversity is a leader in the technology sector trying to do things differently — and succeeding!

So how do we ensure a workplace makes people feel included?

The onboarding process needs to be personalised, managers need to make a point of taking a lot of time to engage with their team members, especially when they work remotely. It is important to understand that supervisors need to increase the variation of contact and the frequency of connecting with their new staff during their first month of employment. Taking on a deliberate strategy to ensure that they operate more like a 'family' — checking in with people when they have been unwell or had other family challenges. Ensuring that the members of your C-Suite recognise that without their people, they don't have a business, so the wellbeing of their people is the number one priority of your business.

The effectiveness of this people-centred approach will create dividends in staffing statistics. Recruiting for diversity, ensuring that your team has the cross section of technical expertise and soft skills needed to be successful, with oversight from a 'people manager', means the needs of the individual team members are balanced between deadlines and the management of their personal lives. This ensures staff are afforded significant flexibility in their work schedule and personal appointments are given priority. By providing all staff with block-out periods where no meetings are scheduled, it enables staff to focus on the work at hand.

This approach to building your team will result in people reporting high levels of job satisfaction, but more than that, they will feel like they work with people who really care about them. From the top down, this ensures that a company's guiding principles are not just nice fodder for their office wall, but a genuine approach that is felt by all staff.

Change in workplace culture is often driven by leaders who have personal experience of challenging workplace cultures, who make a clear and deliberate decision to create a very different working environment for their people.

This is the desire of Luli and the team at TechDiversity and perhaps with a focus similar to what has been outlined above, much like the senior leaders at Google, you may be able to change your workplace for the better.

The solution

Many organisations, inside and outside these sectors, have approached the issue of improved psychological safety in the workplace from a mental health first aid (MHFA) perspective. There is an assumption that completing training in MHFA builds a level of mental health literacy, but that doesn't necessarily translate. MHFA training often raises awareness of the psychological challenges that we observe in others, but it doesn't necessarily increase self-awareness in participants.

The challenge is that the key to better outcomes that reduce the notion of a 'leadership lottery' are about building true mental health literacy, affording the leader the ability to show compassion, demonstrate confidence around psychological safety and enhance their ability to effectively communicate.

For many in these sectors, those types of leaders are like unicorns.

Recent research examined leaders who had personal experiences of mental health challenges, either personally or in their family or friends, and found that these leaders demonstrated better understanding, more compassion, and they felt more confident that they understood more about mental health challenges. These leaders' ability to reach out and communicate with their affected people is ten times higher than in a leader who hasn't recognised those things within themselves, and who hold some level of personal stigma against mental health challenges.

This is something that we can actually assess for. All leadership applicants should be given an assessment of people skills and mental health literacy before being promoted into a leadership position. If we screen for these attributes, it is more likely to lead to positive interactions at some point in the future. Many organisations believe that it creates an additional complication to the recruitment process, however, I would argue that it is a much more effective assessment tool than the subjective assessment of a story that is shared in an interview process.

If you are interested to assess your own mental health literacy and people skills please head to https://kerryannhoward.com/compassionate-leadership-scorecard/ and take the assessment.

Community-based trauma

The black summer bushfires, the pandemic and the 2022 floods in Australia are what I describe as community-based trauma. The benefit of community-based traumatic experiences is that the fact that they affect many members of the community at the same time, rather than just one person, means that they have a mediating affect. It's an easier traumatic process to resolve because I can see that I am not the only one affected, so the standard individual psychological responses to trauma around 'responsibility' are minimised, and the perceived 'lack of control' is widespread. It's a grief process, but it's communal grief.

When we are exposed to a traumatic event as an individual, the impact is mediated by whether or not we feel responsible and, therefore, defective, or whether we had any control over the situation. This is the thing about PTSD development that people don't understand: when we talk about a situation that a person might face on a daily basis, why does one person develop PTSD and another person doesn't? The first risk factor is the perception of responsibility as a contributing factor to the outcome, and the second is the 'natural order' of things.

We know that there are certain things within the community that are wrong: the death of a child is a particularly strong one, unnecessary outcomes from criminal acts is another. The areas that create moral problems — where innocent people are harmed — go against the moral compass and they cause empathic wounds. There are traffic light incidents in all industry sectors. If certain moral circumstances are met, then a person is guaranteed to have a very strong emotional response to that.

In addition, there is an opportunity to intervene early, to assess a person's psychological risk around their perception of responsibility. In any situation, if a person feels like they did something wrong, they are going to have a negative response to it. They may not want to report it, because maybe they didn't follow a process or something. The awareness of this tendency towards responsibility when we conduct a post-incident debrief, provides an opportunity for early intervention. When we review the process, which is pretty standard operational procedure, looking at where things broke down and what is needed for improvement in terms of training, etc. When we identify an error, that is an opportunity to mandate a check-in with the affected people about how they are feeling about it. The quicker we can address these perceptions of responsibility, the greater the chance we have to minimise the traumatic impact on the individual.

Empathy and the leadership lottery

As discussed in chapter 3, a big part of what people report about traumatic experiences in the work environment is heavily dependent on the kind of manager they have. Their mental health awareness and their people-management skills are really the basis of whether a worker might report an incident or not.

The leader's lack of understanding, lack of empathy, lack of ability to engage, communicate and reassure appropriately is a really big challenge for first responders, because they work their way through the leadership continuum by being excellent technicians. They are experts in their field in their ability to control a fire ground or a crime scene, but this is technical expertise that has nothing to do with empathy. The ability to empathise is often referred to as 'soft skills' in this sector, but I would argue that they are 'people skills', and they are essential to managing people.

Leadership isn't about the ability to manage the technicalities of a battlefield, it's about recognising the challenges that the operational environment can have on our humanness. As with many industries, we need to move away from promoting the technical experts into team leader roles. We need a different structure that involves differing attributes in our leadership, not just the command and control environment that is essential for campaigns. The person giving orders in the field doesn't have to be the same person who checks in on your wellbeing, but they need to have some level of understanding of how these experiences may impact future performance.

First responders put their lives on the line day in, day out. It's a very robust environment. They feel they have to be strong all the time, for everyone. If they show vulnerability or some weakness, they would be concerned with how the leadership would perceive that. It's essential that these organisations develop and evolve the people skills of their leadership.

The education component of this has to start at recruitment and be reinforced through the leadership continuum.

The importance of compassionate people leadership

The notion of people leadership is not out of sync with the AIIMS approach. It provides recognition that there is the operational leader, and it's important that they're able to follow direction and they know whose orders they have to follow. In addition, if there was a dedicated people leader who's in control of making sure that their people are really okay, all the time, not just a tick and flick after a particular incident, then this would afford the sector with a truly compassionate leadership solution.

We want to avoid the notion of the leadership lottery. That it's basically hit and miss on whether or not you are going to get the right support if you experience a particularly challenging situation, or you are injured in some form or another. The problem with these sectors is that the assessment of the impact is strongly influenced by the experience of the leader. If the leader perceives that they have been in a similar situation and handled it well, then they can inadvertently diminish the experience of their team member.

We need to eliminate the 'chance' effect that is the leadership lottery

---

It's, unfortunately, part of our human nature to compare ourselves with the person who is telling us their story and put ourselves in the same position. We naturally do this to enable us to feel empathy, but we also use it to assess the validity of the person's experience. This is fraught with difficulty because we all have different backgrounds and experiences that result in different triggers.

Let's consider the position of a firefighter, which is not dissimilar to an infantry soldier, who performs a physically demanding and challenging role, but who also needs to be resilient because of what they are exposed to in their line of work. Their role is to put themself into a physical position of potential harm, usually for some 'greater good'. By fighting this fire, they might save lives. By attacking an enemy, they might protect a group of innocent people.

The impact on the individual and their ability to perform their role can be significant. If there is a significant fear of 'I can't get on that truck' or 'I can't put my breathing apparatus on', if they can't do those basic things, then they start to believe they can't remain a member of the team. These roles operate on a team construct. The perception is that if they cannot keep pace with the other members of the team, then they are going to lose their job. At the same time, there is also the additional worry that the individual takes responsibility for: 'I'm not doing as well as I could and I'm not reporting it. Am I putting my team members at risk?'

These are complex challenges for the individual to consider, but if the member doesn't believe that the organisation can work with them and support them, including providing access to services so they can move into treatment and recovery, then that adds to the stigma and lack of disclosure.

Empowerment

We often hear the term 'self-determination' thrown around in relation to groups of people who are viewed as a minority, such as particular indigenous cultures or disabled persons — the premise being that we need to allow the marginalised group to self-determine what is the right thing for them.

The idea of self-determination has grown from a theory originally proposed by two psychologists back in 1985.[37,38] The premise is that people are able to become self-determined when their needs for competence, connection and autonomy are fulfilled. There are two key assumptions of the theory:

- **The need for growth drives behaviour:** The idea that people are actively directed toward growth. Gaining mastery over challenges and new experiences is essential for developing a cohesive sense of self.

- **Autonomous motivation is important:** Although people may be motivated to act by external rewards, such as money or acclaim (extrinsic motivation), the self-determination theory focuses primarily on internal drivers, such as a need for knowledge or independence (intrinsic motivation).

According to the self-determination theory, in order to achieve psychological growth, an individual requires:

- **Autonomy:** To feel in control of their own behaviours and goals. The ability to take direct action resulting in real change helps people feel self-determined.

- **Competence:** To gain mastery of tasks and learn different skills. The feeling that they possess the skills for success; they take actions that will help them achieve their goals.

- **Connection:** To experience a sense of belonging and attachment to others. As I write in *The Trouble With Trauma*, we need connection to survive.

The challenge with psychological injuries that result in a claim for workers compensation is that the interactions with the insurer afford the injured worker absolutely *no* self-determination. So is it really any surprise that the process of obtaining action validation for any injury is, by its very nature, a completely disenfranchising process?

Social change

There is the argument, which has its roots somewhere back in history, about the needs of the individual versus the needs of the collective. The rights of one group to assume some power over another has been the basis for war since the dawn of time. However, as we have grown and matured as a people, we have started to understand how things have been approached differently in different parts of the world.

We have come to understand that our approach to colonisation over indigenous cultures was wrong, and in many countries, we have sought to introduce self-determination measures as a means to rebalance the power differential for marginalised groups.

We have recognised the prejudice that we have applied to many areas of life (religion, race, gender, sexual orientation, ability) is discriminatory, and we have attempted to correct history by enabling self-determination for these groups. When we look over the various areas that have been encompassed by anti-discrimination laws, we see varying levels of recognition that were achieved over time.

Any social change requires leadership: someone prepared to speak openly about the injustice. This then creates a groundswell effect where others lend their voice to the cause to create political pressure to change. What we then see is a social phenomenon where we swing from 'that never happens' to 'it's everywhere', before we settle into a general state of acceptance that the injustice may happen sometimes, and we need to put things in place to minimise the likelihood of it happening again.

This process has been repeated time and again over our history, and with the emergence of the world wide web and improving technologies, the ebbs and flows of social change have been sped up over the past 30 years. However, sometimes the legal process takes much longer to catch-up.

It's also important to note that these social change constructs relied on a small group coming together as a voice for change. In the case of injured workers, they are marginalised to the extreme by their circumstances and the shame that is created by the failure of the system to afford them recognition validation and self-determination.

This has to change.

CHAPTER 8

Insurance

How to change the outcomes with attitude

The majority of this book has been written to avoid the impact of workers compensation insurance, national insurance, injury insurance in different parts of the world it is known by different names) — in essence it is the insurance that an employer pays to cover the costs of a worker being injured at work, either psychologically or physically.

I wrote this book to try and prevent the development of psychological injuries, because we all know that prevention is 100 times better than the cure. However, in the case of psychosocial injuries, there are some very important reasons why we want to focus on prevention by improving the psychological safety of our work environments.

In the first instance, it is about saving your business money on insurance premiums. Insurance companies are very good at ensuring that they are covered for their risk, so if you have several claims for psychosocial injuries, your premiums will increase significantly. The main reason for this is because the costs of psychological injury are significantly higher than any other type of injury, both in lost time and the cost of treatment to support recovery.

Research highlights that injured worker's experience significantly more negative outcomes once they start interacting with an insurance company.[39] In most cases, this is because the system itself is disenfranchising for the worker. Most insurance companies require the injured worker to 'prove' liability, rather than the employer to 'disprove' liability. In this way, the person who is already suffering from a mental health condition is expected to advocate for themselves, and in most cases, they are expected to do this without an advocate.

In Australia, injured workers are generally not able to utilise the services of a lawyer to support them in making a claim until the liability has been denied. In this way, many insurance companies almost set the injured worker up to fail. Without support, it is very difficult for an injured worker to have the cognitive functioning to complete all of the paperwork required to submit a claim. When their application is denied liability, something that often happens in the case of psychological injury claims, that has a significant impact on their recovery.

Validation

You will recall in chapter 5, I outlined the need to provide validation to the injured worker. If you remember, there are two types of validation: action validation and recognition validation. Insurance companies focus purely on the action validation when assessing a claim; they never offer the injured worker any recognition validation. You will also recall that recognition validation is essential to managing the psychological response, so undergoing the process of an insurance claim results in the injured worker feeling invalidated.

The problem with this invalidation is that it can create a bigger problem for the injured worker. It leads the injured worker down a negative narrative loop that results in a bigger traumatic injury.

Refer back to the earlier explanation in chapter 2 of how events become traumatic. As traumatic events they become stuck in the memory network, and the injured worker gets caught in a constant loop of invalidation.

As a result, they seek validation from a number of other sources, usually from their family and friends or perhaps their work colleagues. If they are afforded recognition validation from external sources, but not afforded action validation by the employer or the insurer, this creates a cognitive dissonance.

> **Cognitive dissonance:** Where a person experiences inconsistent beliefs or thoughts, especially in relation to behavioural decisions and attitude change.

Depending on their other psychological resources, the injured worker will seek action validation from an independent source, in most cases the insurer, and if this doesn't provide the action validation, they may escalate to an advocate who can argue for them, usually a lawyer. You will note how this process just provides an ever-escalating path of seeking action validation from external sources; the longer this is denied, the worse the psychological impact for the injured worker. In this way, the process of making an insurance claim often compounds the impact of the injury.

This scenario is made much worse when the insurance company obtains evidence to deny the claim from the person who was responsible for the injury — it's an irrational process and it usually places the employee and employer in direct conflict about action validation. In Australia, there is no independence to the assessment that would be afforded by an investigative process. In most cases the insurance company doesn't even conduct an investigation. They have an administrative manager who obtains information from the employer about the injured worker's claim, and they compare that to the claim of the injured worker, and often, they will accept the position of the employer in the absence of any evidence to support the employer's claim and deny liability.

All of this is done without any specialised training or investigative skills. The purpose of an investigation is to provide an impartial overview of the facts for a third party to assess liability. At no point is the investigator meant to make a judgement about the liability. Yet, in the absence of any investigation, an insurance claims assessor will take the easiest path to deny liability. They sit as judge, jury and executioner over the livelihood of an injured worker, and they do it utilising a framework that is designed to save the insurance company as much money as possible.

The insurance industry is one of the *most* profitable business sectors, and they like to keep it that way. It's almost a type of insider trading that employees of an insurance company are assessing liability of the claims against itself. It just doesn't seem ethical.

The most effective and efficient, yet profitable, systems of insurance are the 'no fault' systems. Often these are established by government entities, but in the past 40 years, most insurance has been moved to private entities. A no fault system guarantees a minimum of care and aggregates income provision — so when you're injured, you are immediately provided a clear framework of what will be covered and what won't be covered. In this way, you don't have to have an argument about the liability, the insurer doesn't have to pay out money for the administration of the system and both sides save legal costs because they don't need lawyers to argue the case for both sides.

You can understand why neither the insurance industry or the legal profession would be keen to enact such a system, yet, it has been proven to save the insurers money. Further, it has the effect of not exacerbating the psychological impact, because it affords the injured worker recognition validation without any process of action validation taking place.

So why aren't we all doing this?

The legal framework

In countries around the world, the approach to workplace injuries is predominantly based in torts law. Employees around the world have a variety of support options in the event they are injured, from zero support (USA), to government benefits (UK), to a mix of self-insured public entities and private insurance payments (Australia).

This micromanagement of accident compensation increases transaction costs and creates inefficiency and uncertainty.[39] The rationalisation for individual responsibility is that it does more than determine who is compensated. It is thought to deter wrongful behaviour, thus, the United States is thought to be a safer place because of individual responsibility legislation.[39] But is it?

The United States, United Kingdom and Canadian systems are more heavily biased towards individual responsibility for accidents and compensation, with the focus on deterrence of wrongful behaviour.[40] New Zealand operates on a system based on community responsibility for accidents, with the focus on actual compensation for victims. This is based on the findings of The Woodhouse Report, which recommended a pure no-fault scheme. Once a personal injury by accident is identified, compensation is mandated under the Act, and a cause of action in tort is not allowed. For example, in the case of an ordinary negligent automobile collision, both drivers are fully compensated to the extent provided by the Act, regardless of their degree of culpability, and neither can sue the other.

Since many tort scholars believe that one of the more important functions of the tort system is its deterrence of unsafe practices, such as safety with automobiles, construction, landowners, consumer products, and medical treatment. Tort scholars also believe that the tort system promotes individual responsibility and protects individual rights. However, this is a purely legal argument, and doesn't take into consideration the impact of the legal process on the psychological outcomes of the victim.

The New Zealand law incorporated mental injury up until 1992. In fact, one case decided under the 1982 Act, the Court of Appeal said:

It would be a strange situation if cover under the Act for a person suffering serious mental consequences caused by an accident were to depend upon whether or not some physical injury however slight also is sustained. Further it would create major difficulties should it be necessary in particular cases to separate physical and mental injuries.[41]

For some reason, in 1992, this reasonable and rational legal position was overturned. Since then, there has been a significant increase in damages claims for mental trauma using the torts of assault, battery and negligence.[41]

The Australian model

When I started writing this book, I felt that my understanding of the New Zealand model was going to provide a fantastic model for the world. However, their system has become more rejecting of psychological injuries over time, for what appears to be the same reasons that many restrictions have been put in place around mental health — it's too hard to control and appears to be a volatile system that lacks transparency.

I would argue that the mental health of human beings is actually really simple to understand and manage when we recognise that unnecessary judgement and lack of appropriate validation practices are responsible for causing traumatic injuries. I started writing believing that the Australian system was flawed and causing more problems for workers with psychosocial injuries, however, my research would indicate that the Australian system is probably the 'best' in the world currently. So, if the best is still causing significant harm, we have a long way to go to improve outcomes for employees.

The Australian model provides all employers with a national statutory obligation to provide workers compensation insurance for their employees, however, the insurance schemes vary on a state-by-state basis. This is a common legal setting in Australia. As a federation of states, there are nationally binding obligations that are applied differently by each state. This results in differential outcomes for employees depending on which state they work in. As a result, it is better to be an injured worker in Victoria than it is in other states, due to the fact that the Victorian Government has strong regulatory powers and processes — and they enforce them. In many other states, the regulation of the insurance industry is pathetic. Some governments self-insure, including the Federal Government and the Australian Capital Territory (ACT).

The legal position in Australia means that an injured worker can make a workers compensation claim for either a physical or a psychological injury — this is probably the first point in which the system is flawed, as it doesn't readily allow for the natural inclusion of physiological and psychological therapies to facilitate recovery. It is still based on the 'disconnect' of mind and body, despite the fact that research clearly shows that they are strongly correlated!

Recovery can only be facilitated when we address both the physical and the psychological, because our physical injuries carry a psychological component, and psychological injuries can give rise to neurological and inflammatory physical issues. To date, there has been no change to the categorisation of injuries, despite the fact that the law itself says that 'an injury is an injury'.

Once an employee lodges a claim for workers compensation, it goes through a process of action validation, by which the claim is either accepted or rejected. There are only eight insurance companies that underwrite private workers compensation in Australia,[42] yet they apply different rules depending on the state in which the claim is made. The workers compensation insurance schemes are administered by very profitable insurance companies, who ultimately have obligations to their shareholders to turn a profit. As you can appreciate, this means that the administration of the scheme is geared towards reducing the burden on the insurance company.

The assessment of risk is rated by industry, the employer pays premiums based on perceived occupational risk, and if there is a claim of any type, the employers' premiums increase significantly. As such, if a worker is injured in your workplace, your workers compensation premiums will rise and the injured worker's recovery is taken out of your hands. In addition, the system is designed to dissuade employees making claims, due to the stress of the action validation process. So a worker's compensation claim is something that we want to avoid — it's not beneficial for either the employer or the employee.

If an employee's claim is accepted, there is usually an initial 'grace period' whereby the insurer seemingly provides the claimant with significant support and access to services to support recovery. These claims managers are usually paid on a 'bonus' system linked to the time it takes to get an employee back to work. This results in an initial significant concentrated process to help the employee to return to work, until the time related KPI has expired.

Employer contact with injured workers

From the time an employee's claim is accepted, the employer is somewhat isolated from the recovery process. Even in states like New South Wales, where there is a legal requirement for the employer to maintain contact with the employee, this obligation is usually delegated to the human resources area as a key performance indicator to 'tick the box' of making contact with the employee. This process actually causes more harm to the employee, as it results in the employee feeling like a number, not a valued employee.

If there is an investigation into the employer because of the injury, the injured worker's feelings about the employer will be complicated. If a physical injury is the result of equipment failure, the injury is not the worker's fault, the investigation is undertaken by the regulatory body and, eventually, the employer may be found liable for the equipment failure. So how is the employer meant to be able to maintain a 'relationship' with an injured worker when they are legally responsible for their injury? It's counter intuitive.

The obligation to maintain the communication between employer and employee is an admirable notion, one that was designed to provide an injured worker with a sense of value as an employee. I have highlighted this earlier in this book, so why am I now saying that this obligation may create challenges? It's because, depending on the size of the organisation, the legal obligation usually becomes a KPI for the HR team, rather than the immediate supervisor. So, post injury, the worker receives weekly calls from the HR manager, someone they have no personal relationship with, and it feels like a 'tick and flick' duty, leaving the injured worker feeling that it is disingenuous. As a result, they feel even less important to the employer.

When we add to this the complications regarding the potential for an employer being found liable for the equipment failure, is it any surprise that the worker doesn't want to maintain contact with an employer representative? If their immediate supervisor were to maintain regular contact through the first three months of the injury, this would have a very different impact for that worker.

Another problem arises if, in addition to this, the primary contact for the injured worker ends up being the case manager appointed to their insurance claim. In most cases of obvious physical injuries, in the early stages of the injury claim, the case managers are very supportive and helpful. However, there is a lot of turnover in case managers in Australia, and this can prove quite unsettling for the injured worker. It's a very personal connection when you have to ask someone for permission to engage in activities that you, or your health professionals, believe will help you to recover. The case manager becomes the central point of power in the injured worker's recovery. As such, they can do a lot of good, but they can also cause extreme harm.

The process of making a claim for an injury in Australia is very straightforward and simple, but the disenfranchisement that occurs once the claim is accepted is something that needs to change. Australia is unique in its recognition of bullying and harassment in the workplace, however, the system ensures that the injured worker is not likely to recover quickly, especially in the case of a psychosocial injury.

The reason that employers don't like to contact injured workers has a lot to do with fear that they will be accused of making the employee feel worse by being perceived to 'harass' them. This is why the legal obligations tend to be delegated to an independent party in HR, rather than the direct line manager. However, I believe that a lot of the perception can be managed with effective communication.

Depending on the nature of the injury, it may not be appropriate for the point of contact to be the line manager. If the injury is physical, regardless of whether the injury is a workplace or personal injury, it is important that the employee maintains contact with the line manager. However, the communication has to be carefully managed to ensure that it is perceived as empathic support rather than harassment about their recovery time. If the injury is psychological, then it is likely to involve the line manager in some way — either directly or indirectly. As such, the point of contact should be the more senior manager in the reporting line and needs to focus on wellbeing.

In organisations where the employee is well supported and shown empathy when they have been injured, they recover quicker. This is especially true in large organisations where the employee may be able to be accommodated in a different work area. The key here is to promote 'recovery at work'.

The challenge

When I began writing this book, I was coming from the perspective that the Australian system was broken, and there had to be a better way of managing things that improved outcomes for affected individuals.

I understand the Australian context, and I believe that the system has some major faults that actually cause more harm to injured workers. It's really challenging to write this because there are complexities to the Australian system that, although it is meant to support an injured worker and it is one of the few systems in the world that supports psychological injuries, it still doesn't do this in a positive way.

As a psychologist, I have supported injured workers for over a decade, and I have spent a lot of time writing reports to support access to care for injured workers, as well as fighting with insurance companies for access to support for the injured worker. The system is supposed to be more supportive of the injured worker; in terms of getting a claim approved, especially for psychological injuries, it is one of the simplest systems in the world. However, once the insurance company gets involved it creates more problems.

Why? Because the system disenfranchises the injured worker.

Denial

The biggest issue in an insurance claim comes when the employer representatives try to cover up their own inadequacy in processing the claim. I have seen some of the most abhorrent behaviour around legitimate workers compensation claims that are denied by the employer. In most cases, this occurs in areas of whistle-blowing — where the employee pointed out a problem, and the organisation was so embarrassed by the implications that the individual's position is denied all the way up the line. This type of workplace injury is usually only seen in larger organisations, because a smaller business can't afford to ignore the implications of the unethical behaviour that the whistle-blower is trying to raise awareness about.

These types of injury are not going to be caused by readers of this book, because this type of leader has no compassion for their people at all. This leader is self-serving and relentless in their pursuit of the person who dares to hold a mirror up to their unethical behaviour. These are the workplace sociopaths who are often found in the upper echelons of big corporate and public sector entities.

The issue for these injured workers is that the sociopathic behaviour is usually so entrenched in the organisation that when the person finally has to leave the workplace, their experiences continue to be denied by the system that they were trying to fight against. There are several examples of this type of behaviour (some with the potential for public scandal) that I will refer to as the 'headline effect'. This type of behaviour is most commonly seen in public sector entities, where errors are commonly made and always denied.

The issue for the injured internal whistle-blower is that they have often been left to fend for themselves against a system in which they are supposed to be legally protected. In Australia, the strongest whistle-blower protections are afforded to those who are employed by public companies. They include criminal offences and civil penalties for a person causing, or threatening to cause, detriment to a whistle-blower; or breaching a whistle-blower's confidentiality, including during an investigation into the whistle-blower's concerns.

A disclosure of a work-related grievance will only be protected if it relates to systemic issues, or involves detrimental conduct to the whistle-blower. A disclosure of a work-related grievance will also be protected if it is made to a legal practitioner to obtain legal advice or representation in relation to the whistle-blower provisions.[43] These legal protections can create further challenges for the injured whistle-blower because the denial of the unethical behaviour continues to be covered up, often including through the denial of the workers compensation claim.

The obligations for the public sector are not as strong as in the corporate world. Obligations under Section 16 of the *Australian Public Service Act*: 'Protection for whistle-blowers', which prohibits victimisation of, or discrimination against, an Australian Public Service (APS) employee who reports a breach, or an alleged breach, of the code of conduct to an agency head, the public service commissioner or the merit protection commissioner, or persons authorised by them. There are several areas within the public sector in which victimisation is so well known that the lawyers have become very familiar with the modus operandi of the regular offenders.

How the *Safety, Rehabilitation and Compensation Act* affects government workers

The problem with whistle-blowing is that it occurs most commonly in the public sector, a system that is self-insured and self-regulated. It's an insular system that is designed to protect itself and deny, deny, deny! This, of course, results in a system that is self-serving and not supportive of the injured worker.

In Australia, the biggest representative entity is Comcare: the self-insured entity of the federal government. The insurer covers 375 500 workers in Australia, and the *Safety, Rehabilitation and Compensation (SRC) Act*, the legislation governing workers compensation for government employees, also applies to government employees in the Australian Capital Territory (ACT).

Under the *SRC Act*, an employee can lodge a claim for either a physical or psychological injury sustained in the workplace. There is no clear way to accept that an injury is an injury, and shouldn't need to be defined as physical or psychological. Often in cases where the injury is physical, we see a secondary psychological claim arise because of how the injured employee is treated due to the limitations of their physical injury. Recall Karen's story in chapter 6? This is an example of this all too common phenomenon.

The other issue with the *SRC Act* is that it limits the injured worker's ability to access support from a legal representative in the early phases of a claim. In fact, an injured worker is expected to be able to complete the extensive documentation on their own, and they are even expected to interact with the employer's representative, all of which can be triggering for an injured worker, especially in a psychological claim. The system does not allow the injured worker to obtain any sort of advocate until the claim has been denied, and that worker is forced into a situation in which they have to obtain legal support to fight for a review of the decision. All of this takes a significant emotional toll on an already injured worker.

Worse, the system is self-assessing. The review of these decisions is put before a tribunal, rather than a court, which means it is presided over by government-appointed members who have often made significant contributions to political parties through family members, before being appointed to a system that isn't transparent and doesn't follow standard legal process. In addition, the members of administrative tribunals in Australia have some of the lightest caseloads in legal history, and are paid significant amounts of money for very little case finalisation.

Why am I highlighting the politicisation of a legal process? Because these people preside over decisions that cause further harm to injured workers. When an initial claim is lodged, Comcare undertake an assessment that includes obtaining input from the employer representative, and then the case manager makes a determination of whether or not to accept liability. There are policy directives that are made under different political regimes that change the rates of acceptance of liability at the initial claim stage and, not surprisingly, these rates change based on which political party is in power.

Politics should *never* preside over injured workers.

Self-regulating systems are, by their nature, self-serving and, therefore, prone to corruption. Right-wing governments tend to encourage self-protection, and left-wing governments tend to provide better support for the underdog. The world has seen an extended period of right-wing politics, self-serving, dog-eat-dog, and egocentric consumerism. There is very little 'community' in right-wing politics.

The support for injured employees is really a community concern. The self-insurance of injured workers by government has led to the corruption of a system that is legislated to support people who are injured at work. The *SRC Act* allows the government to deny legitimate claims and deny support to workers. Support that is afforded to other injured workers who are employed in private enterprise. The Federal Government sets the legislative framework for workers compensation obligations at a national level, but the administration of the system is managed at state level. This is why the outcome of a workers compensation injury for the worker is better in the Northern Territory or Victoria than it is in the ACT or NSW.

Which system is the best?

Intuitively, I believe that the best psychological outcomes will be achieved by elimination of the opportunity to deny a claim, therefore, by the provision of a 'no fault' insurance system.

The obligations in the Northern Territory are unique because they provide a no-fault workers compensation system for all workplace injuries, regardless of whether the injury is physical or psychological. Interestingly, you will note in table 8.1 that the Northern Territory is the only jurisdiction that has lowered their percentage of claims involving mental stress over the past decade — I suspect that this may be related to their 'no fault' system.

Table 8.1: Proportion of serious claims involving mental stress by jurisdiction.

Proportion of Claims (%)	2014–15	2015–16	2016–17	2017–18	2018–19	2019–20p
VIC	8.7	9.1	9.8	9.9	11.9	12.0
SA	9.4	6.3	9.2	8.5	11.2	11.2
Aus Gov	13.9	12.5	11.9	13.7	12.4	11.0
NSW	5.9	6.8	7.7	9.7	10.8	9.5
TAS	7.2	8.2	9.1	8.8	9.5	9.4
ACT	6.2	6.3	7.0	7.1	7.2	8.1
QLD	3.1	3.4	3.6	3.5	4.3	4.8
NT	5.3	5.5	4.2	3.3	4.5	4.5
WA	2.7	2.9	2.8	3.1	3.6	3.5
Seacare	0.8	4.1	4.3	4.2	2.8	3.3
Australian Average	5.8	6.1	6.7	7.4	8.6	8.4

Source: Safe Work Australia © Commonwealth of Australia.

The New Zealand model is also a no-fault model, however, the automatic provision for psychological injuries was removed 1992.

In Queensland, changes enacted in 2021 have moved to a 'presumption of injury' for first responders who have been diagnosed with PTSD. Other psychological injuries require proof that the employment provided a significant contributing factor. The impact of the changes on presumption for first responders is still too early to be clearly correlated.

The entitlements that are applied to an injured worker in Victoria are more consistent, more supportive of their recovery, and the regulator takes the enforcement of penalties against an employer very seriously, in addition to the fact that they have a rigorous process of independent investigation and enforcement of legal obligations on the insurer.

It is a well-known fact in Australia that Victoria is the state to live in for access to community services. Why? Because Victoria has a large population-density rate in comparison to the rest of Australia. It is simply easier to get the balance right when you have population-density concentration over a small geographic area. However, it also has a reasonably strong 'middle ground' of political attitudes over many years. Throughout the pandemic, the government was able to wield unprecedented political control over the population to prevent movement and control population health. This was only possible because of the integration of the public safety sector in Victoria.

The issue for workers in other states is that the regulatory enforcement over employers and insurance companies is inadequate and inconsistent. There is no impetus to force change either. Federal Government employees are disadvantaged, depending on which superannuation system their employment is tied to. About ten years ago, the government enforced an additional layer of insurance cover over government employees for income protection insurance, which must be taken with an external insurance company. This affords injured workers some financial security that enables them to be paid through income protection while the Comcare system denies their claim. Under this system, they are even afforded superannuation payments for up to five years post injury — something that is denied them under the *SRC Act*.

It would appear that the Government recognised the inadequacy of its own systems, but rather than fixing them, they took the easier route of enforcing an insurance obligation on workers to cover themselves. No doubt, a class action regarding lost superannuation payments for injured workers covered by the *SRC Act* will present itself in the near future. All states have adopted obligations regarding superannuation contributions for injured workers in the past decade, it's about time the Federal Government got aligned.

But enough of the politics... What happens to the worker when the claim is denied?

Well, not surprisingly, their psychological outcomes are far worse. The duration of the injury stops being months and turns into years. The process of appealing an administrative decision alone takes over 12 months, and regularly results in continued denial of the claim, prolonging the injury even further. On appeal, this may be overturned in a proper court system that follows due legal process, but the negative outcomes for the injured worker are often permanent by this stage, and it is not uncommon to have lost five years of their life in the process. As you can see from the tables 8.3 and 8.3 — there are huge differences in the recovery from mental health injuries versus all other injuries.

Table 8.2: Serious workers' compensation claims and median time lost for mental health conditions, 2015–16 to 2019–20p.

Financial year	Serious claims	Median time lost (working weeks)
2015–16	6915	18.8
2016–17	7819	20.8
2017–18	8679	23.9
2018–19	10 429	26.6
2019–20p	10 776	

Source: Safe Work Australia's National Dataset for Compensation-based Statistics. © Commonwealth of Australia.

Table 8.3: Serious workers' compensation claims and median time lost for all injuries/diseases excluding mental health conditions, 2015–16 to 2019–20p.

Financial year	Serious claims	Median time lost (working weeks)
2015–16	99 509	5.4
2016–17	100 017	5.8
2017–18	102 952	6
2018–19	105 278	6.4
2019–20p	109 579	

Source: Safe Work Australia's National Dataset for Compensation-based Statistics. © Commonwealth of Australia.

Erin's story

Erin is a dog-handling law enforcement officer who has been on the job for over ten years. Erin has seen a lot in her time, but constantly finds that speaking up about ethical concerns is pointless because her observations are regularly denied as a weakness of her gender: 'Stop being such a girl!'

In denying her observations of animal mistreatment, the employer representatives continue to protect the offenders. Even when investigations provide evidence of unethical behaviour, the 'club' closes ranks around the offenders and scapegoats the whistle-blower. The lack of workplace safety is well-known, and Erin is informed that she cannot be in the workplace alone. When Erin lodges a claim for workers compensation, the same leadership denies the claims of workplace safety and, instead, turns the claim around, indicating poor performance on Erin's part. The employer's claim is completely lacking in evidence, but, nevertheless, supported by the insurer and Erin's claim is denied.

The challenge of the assessment process in a case like Erin's is in the policy position of the insurer — they add more weight to the employer's position, rather than accepting the employee's claims. An employee is required to provide evidence of the lack of workplace safety through emails, conversations, observations — all backed up with medical evidence of the impact of this on the injured worker over time. Yet, the employer's representative can provide a statement that denies the evidence, and makes a red herring claim for why the worker is injured, without actually providing any supporting evidence. The employer's position is accepted without evidence, and the claim is denied. All of this takes place without the injured worker being afforded any legal support or advocacy.

Especially in the case of a psychological injury, the expectation that a person can advocate for themselves is completely unrealistic. Cognitively, the person is struggling, so their memory is impaired, and they are often struggling with sleep issues and low mood, so they find it very difficult to function and attend to their daily needs, let alone find the energy to mount another fight against their employer.

The system is geared to further alienate injured workers, yet is promoted as the system that protects them. I think this is where Australia's seemingly 'supportive' system actually creates a worse outcome for the injured worker. At least in the United States, you expect the system will support the employer and, therefore, people move on quicker to some other form of employment. However, in Australia we are educated to believe that, as workers, we are protected against bullying and harassment in the workplace. In fact, our legal system provides protection against it, but the regulatory system usually does not enforce the protection of the injured worker.

In Erin's case, her claim is made under the *SRC Act,* so her claim has to be escalated through the tribunal to be resolved. However, as we have already identified, the tribunal process is politicised, and the likelihood that Erin's claim will succeed in the tribunal is dependent on the member presiding over the matter. The awareness of this bias is so well known in the legal profession that lawyers will start preparing the avenues for appeal based on who is hearing the case.

While the case is being prepared, and the time delays of the administrative processes plod along, Erin may be left without income, depending on her own personal circumstances. In this case, she fell under the new system that forced her to take out income protection insurance through her public sector superannuation scheme. As such, she was able to lodge a claim with the income protection insurer, a private insurance entity. They accepted her claim, and they are currently paying her and contributing to superannuation on her behalf, and they will continue to do so until the administrative process either accepts or denies her claim, up to a maximum of five years.

If the administrative review process accepts her claim, then the private insurer will be reimbursed by Comcare for all of the support services, treatments, income payments and superannuation contributions made on Erin's behalf while the claim and the appeal were being heard. This private system affords Erin much better access to services and treatments that are designed to support her recovery, and her superannuation benefits have not been negatively impacted by her injury. Arguably, Erin's chances of recovery from her injury are much higher under the private income protection insurer than they are under the government insurance scheme.

The sceptic in me periodically thinks that perhaps the government recognised the failings of its own system and chose to require its employees to self-insure, rather than take the steps necessary to improve the scheme for its members. I live in hope that this oversight will be resolved at some point in the near future.

So if the denial of a claim prolongs the injury and practically eliminates the chance that an injured worker will ever recover, why do we continue to invalidate claims?

Policy directives to save money

No doubt, some government actuary ran the numbers and decided that the goal is to initially deny the claims to save money. Certainly, there was a policy decision post the 2016 election, when Australia changed to a Liberal government, for Comcare to review all of its long-term claims and move to deny liability in the hopes of saving money. It is common for Liberal governments to reduce the balance sheet in the public service. Sometimes this involves some creative accounting, like denying long-term claimants, and forcing them into an administrative review process to have their claims re-assessed. At the same time, the administrative review tribunal has been stacked with political appointments who proceed to deny claims, and creatively find legal ways to close down opportunities for proper judicial review.

It would take a much more in-depth forensic accounting process to determine the actual 'savings' that were achieved through these policy decisions. In reality, the balance sheet may have shown savings in the number of 'post-45 week' injured workers claims, however, the increased resourcing of the Australian Government solicitor's office wouldn't be on the same balance sheet.

As a result of the politicisation of the review process, many claims were denied liability, and there was little opportunity for appeal. The Australian legal system is very rigid in terms of the legal process that is required for a case to progress. In essence, an appeal can only be made to a higher legal authority on points of law. So, a very creative member of an administrative tribunal can deny a claim, and write it up in such a way that it denies the individual any opportunity to appeal. You can't just appeal a decision because you don't agree with it, there has to be a clear argument that highlights the factual inaccuracy of application of the law by the member before an appeal can be made to a higher court. Even then, the individual has to have the means to continue the legal process.

An appeal to the Magistrates Court to appeal a decision by the Administrative Appeals Tribunal will cost in excess of $7000 just in the filing fee. Then there are usually expert witness statements and other legal disbursements that are necessary to appeal to a higher court. Then you need to have a legal representative who will either take it on pro bono or you have to also find the funds to pay your legal representatives. Thankfully, Australia has a significant number of firms who operate on a 'no win, no fee' basis for these types of cases, yet they don't usually operate on that basis for the Administrative Appeals Tribunal in the first instance. This is because the politicisation of the system means that it is legally too unpredictable for the lawyer to bank on their own legal assessment of the claim.

As you can see, the implications for an injured worker at this end of the system are extremely damaging. Most can only survive it with a very supportive legal team and good interpersonal, familial and social support.

Even then, the psychological damage is excessive, and the system somehow manages to avoid the negligence liability of putting a person through such a process. When an appeal overturns the decision of the Administrative Appeals Tribunal to uphold Comcare's right to deny ongoing liability in the claim, the court has no power to grant the injured worker any damages for the psychological damage created by the negligence of the insurer in denying liability in the first place.

The decision of the higher court is merely to uphold the right of the injured worker to the claim, and the *SRC Act* doesn't have any time-enforcement obligations on the insurer. As a result, Comcare have to reinstate the injured worker's access to entitlements, but they can take their time doing it.

In my own case against Comcare,[44] the Federal Court overturned the decision in July, and it took Comcare seven months to reinstate payments. So, when the 'fight' was over and I won, it actually wasn't over because the Court didn't have the power to force the insurer to do anything because the *SRC Act* is Federal Court legislation that sits outside the legal system in terms of the usual torts of law, which are generally created by common law.

The *SRC Act* codifies the worker's compensation regime. The *SRC Act* also created a threshold, by way of a level of permanent impairment, that a worker must overcome before they are entitled to pursue their common law rights to sue their employer for negligence and damages. The *SRC Act* also requires workers to give up any further entitlements they may have under the Act if they choose to pursue their common law rights. That choice, once made, is irrevocable, meaning the worker cannot return to claim statutory entitlements even if their common law claim is unsuccessful.

The Commonwealth, via the *SRC Act,* and almost all states and territories (except the ACT) now have statutory workers compensation legislation that curtails workers compensation rights. Those curtailments vary across all schemes, however, generally include:

- capping and limiting a worker's entitlements

- excluding the need for insurers (or their employers) to pay superannuation entitlements to an injured worker

- excluding a worker's ability to access common law rights to sue their employer unless they reach a statutorily prescribed level of permanent impairment

- requiring an injured worker to agree to forgo any future workers compensation entitlements if they choose to pursue common law rights, even if they are unsuccessful in doing so.

As we can see, the obligations on the Commonwealth are fewer than is now standard in many states and territories, especially in the non-payment of superannuation and the prevention of access to common law. As such, the Federal Government can make policy decisions that negatively affect individuals, and may ultimately be found to be negligent, but they can avoid obligations to the individual under torts law because the legislation sits outside it.

Many people think that being a public servant is a really easy job with good pay and conditions. However, most people are not aware that when things go wrong, the individual has fewer rights than they would if they were employed by a private entity in Australia. I'm not clear about the public vs private sector in other countries, certainly the private sector outcomes for the individual are far worse in more right-wing politicised countries, such as the United States, where the laws in each state vary, but are heavily geared in favour of the employer.

How and where regulation is enforced

What is clear is that the denial of a claim costs the system a lot more than it saves. Private insurers have recognised this, and so the rates of acceptance of claims in the private sector are much higher. Firstly, most private insurers have claims investigated before deciding on liability. In states where the regulatory body is very active, workplace injuries are often investigated by the regulator.

WorkSafe Victoria appears to be the most proactive regulator of workers compensation law in Australia. WorkSafe delivers many programs and proactively targets early intervention with both injured workers and employers in an attempt to reduce the time that a worker is out of the workplace.

WorkSafe Victoria employs over 200 inspectors and around 60 investigators, and their inspectors are key to compliance. Inspectors are able to issue infringement notices to employers on the spot, which provides a significant deterrent effect and steers employers to safety compliance. Improvement notices and prohibition notices can become costly exercises for employers who are required to fix systems of work, plant and governance before resuming work in specific areas.

WorkSafe Victoria has many initiatives and targeted interventions for injured workers, and supporting the employee to return to work. In addition, it delivers a breadth of education to employers. There are many proactive initiatives that incorporate legislative changes, such as the recent 'OHS (Psychological Health) Regulations (PHRegs)' which are currently under review by the Victorian Government and are proposed to commence in early 2023.

The proposed amendments will provide guidance to employers on their obligations to protect workers from mental injury. They make it clear that hazards posing a risk to psychological health are as harmful to worker health and wellbeing as physical hazards.

The new obligations will apply to any employer who has 50 or more employees, and will include new definitions to support employers' understanding of psychosocial hazards. This legislation will set a new global standard in workers compensation outcomes for workers with psychosocial injuries, and it will be enforced by the powers of a substantial regulator.

Any workplace injury is required to be reported under law. WorkSafe claims are managed by a dedicated business unit, and aligned with other units that look at aspects connected to claims, from fraud by employees during claims payments to breaches by employers for failure to report incidents subject to claims. Providers can also be investigated for fraud or other potential breaches. WorkSafe can elect to look at fraudulent claims or claims where there is maladministration, including agent performance.

The investigation of claims is mostly a decision made by insurance agents who have the authority to appoint licensed companies to provide factual investigations — the process of action validation to inform decisions around liability by the insurer. In other states, the workers compensation insurers engage subcontractor investigators to undertake workplace investigations when a claim for compensation is lodged.

Under the *SRC Act,* there is no such regulatory review process enforced to independently investigate the claims of the injured worker. So public sector workers are not afforded the protection of an independent review, merely a desktop review by a case manager who is following a politicised process. There is no action validation nor is there any recognition validation — there is no validation for the injured worker at all. Rather, the denial of the experience of the injured worker continues to erode the mental health of the worker in a system that has no consequences for their negligence.

So how can we force change in the public sector?

It needs to change because these costs are being funded by the taxpayer. In the ACT, the disproportionate burden of government means that 5 per cent of the population is employed by the ACT Government, and the injury rates are similar to the federal government. Up until a few years ago, ACT Government claims were assessed and administered by Comcare, when the ACT Government decided that the cost of Comcare administration and the poor outcomes meant that they would be better off using a private insurer to administer the scheme.

They now outsource the management of the workers compensation scheme, still under the *SRC Act,* to a private insurer, with the expectation that the private insurer would provide better management of the scheme, reduce costs and get people back to work sooner. However, due to the scheme being governed by the *SRC Act,* the process of assessing claims hasn't improved; rather the private insurer has adopted the policy of 'denying' claims in the first instance. The bottom line on the balance sheet may have improved, but the outcomes for the injured worker continue to deteriorate.

The biggest gains could be made in a jurisdiction like the ACT because of its legislative position. It's a small community, with a lot of public sector infrastructure. The ability to adopt many of the recommendations that I have outlined in this book and apply them to the public sector would be easy to do in the ACT. Such a program could redefine workers compensation schemes the world over, by proving the benefits of a no-fault system that maintains engagement with injured workers and supports their recovery at work.

Why the insurance system makes it worse

If you consider all of the elements that I have discussed in the book, you will recognise that there are multiple ways to improve the way we interact with each other that will prevent challenges in the workplace. Once an insurance company is involved, employers are often left in the dark about the process of recovery for their employee. Payments to the employees are usually handled by the insurer, so the employer only becomes involved once there is an opportunity for the employee to return to work in some capacity.

This is where things become overly complicated, and I think this is where the Australian system fails injured workers. The legal implications of workplace injuries often create a sense of 'learned helplessness' in the employee. If there is any sort of legal process, the lawyers will often recommend that the injured worker not do anything to jeopardise the potential for compensation, so there can be a level of secondary gain for the worker in not returning to the workplace. It's important to recognise that this is *sometimes* the case, but employer attitudes in Australia seem to indicate that *all* injured workers are malingering.

I spoke earlier about the cynicism that can develop around injured workers. I have heard many HR managers talk about how injured workers are just malingering, bunging it on or lazy! It's important to define malingering here because the perception that I hear a lot is not actually a true reflection of the term 'malingering'. Firstly, is it crucial to understand that malingering is not a continuously 'present' or 'absent' phenomenon. Malingering is categorised into four types:

- invention of symptoms

- perseveration, or describing symptoms that previously existed

- exaggeration of real symptoms

- transference, or attributing real symptoms to a false cause.[45, 46]

Amongst health practitioners, there is a general consensus that the perception of malingering in injured workers is over-estimated. Reflecting back on our recruitment strategies, there is even testing that seems to pre-screen potential employees for the likelihood of malingering known as 'integrity testing'.[45, 46] There is, however, a real challenge with learned helplessness amongst injured workers.

The medical profession can sometimes enable this behaviour, particularly in situations where the injured worker has been psychologically harmed. I get the need to support injured workers, but it needs to be done in a system that supports recovery, rather than aiding avoidance. In order to do this effectively, a detailed assessment of the barriers to work has to be completed.

Nowhere in the world is there a system that embraces holistic recovery for injured workers. There needs to be a dedicated problem-solving resource that works with the injured worker to overcome the challenges that prevent participation: an empowerment model that provides the injured worker with a sense of purpose for moving forward and supports them with a plan for recovery.

This holistic model needs to incorporate all elements of the injured worker's situation. It needs to afford them a safe working environment to support the worker to test their abilities and their limitations: a supported employment model that encourages the injured worker to test their capacity for meaningful work. This model should be funded by the insurance company, rather than the employer, as it is about supporting recovery rather than creating a bigger burden on the employer's resources.

This is especially important for long-term injured workers who are unable to return to their previous employer for whatever reason. The biggest barrier to their ability to find gainful employment elsewhere is the perception of risk that has to be assumed by the new employer. If there was a limited period of risk that was assumed by the insurer, to support the injured worker to ease into a new role, say a period of six to 12 months, then we may find ourselves in a situation where these injured workers can recover.

I find it frustrating that the insurance system doesn't provide any support or incentives for a new employer to employ an injured worker. In terms of cost benefits, it would save the insurance company a significant amount of money in the long-term, and it would afford the injured worker some opportunity to recover. There needs to be incentives and support provided to enable such a system to be implemented.

CHAPTER 9

Prevention

The 'recovery at work' early intervention model

There are many reasons why, as leaders, we should seek to continuously improve the approach our workplace has towards its people. There are many things that we can do to improve things in our own workplaces, but there are also some systemic changes that would be beneficial to adopt in workplaces around the globe.

Recovery at work model

In terms of lost work time, psychological injuries result in the longest time off work, and they are the most costly injuries. In addition, many employees who suffer physical injuries (either from their work or personally) have their recovery negatively impacted by the inevitable psychological stress that results from feelings of physical pain, in addition to the shame of being injured and the disconnection from the workplace. Any physical therapist will tell you that stress prolongs recovery due to the complex neurobiological responses that traumatic experiences create in our bodies.

Stress increases inflammation in the body and prolongs recovery due to our complex neurobiological response to trauma

Employers are conflicted about how to support employees to recover because of the perceived conflict between the medical practitioners assessment of the employee's work capacity and the resulting legal obligation on the employer. We need to balance the needs of the employee to recover by providing the right support to facilitate it.

Much of the perceived conflict can be managed in the initial onboarding of a new staff member. When we tell people what they can expect from us as employers if they become ill or injured *before* they become injured, the employee feels less pressured when they are contacted by the employer when they are off work.

It's as simple as setting expectations ...

The issue is that many employers don't want to talk about what they will do for the employee if they become ill or injured, because they fear setting up an expectation in the employee to be injured! It's a strange, almost superstitious ideology that humans have developed, that implies that if we don't talk about it, it won't happen. This is a form of heuristic bias called an illusory correlation, a term first coined by psychology Professor Loren J. Chapman (1927–). Illusory biases can lead to stereotyping.[47]

I have worked with many organisations who baulk at the idea of speaking openly about how they will handle potentially negative events in the future — it's as if by talking about it, we will manifest it. Yet, the opposite is true. When we discuss obligations under 'employee wellbeing', the employee feels more valued by the employer, and will be open to employer approaches when they become ill for any reason.

Psychologically, we do not resist something when we know about it. When we set expectations of the approach before it is required, there is no psychological perception of being approached any differently to what we expect.

So, when we tell our new recruit that we really value their health and wellbeing, and to support it we have a contact requirement for illness or injury, they expect the contact and welcome it.

We explain to them that if they become ill for any reason, their line manager is going to make contact with them to ask after their health daily for the first three days, then after one week, and then twice a week if they are off work for an extended period. This contact will be by telephone, and if they employee can't be reached, the employer will continue to attempt to make contact to ensure that they are okay. If, for any reason, the direct supervisor is not the appropriate person to make this contact, then this contact will be made by the next senior line manager. This is in no way about pressuring an employee, on the contrary it is because we know that feeling valued and supported by your employer really supports people to feel less stressed when ill or injured, and this supports employee recovery.

Then the line manager has to follow through with these phone calls, often best made at the end of the work day. During this call, the manager should *never* ask when the employee will be returning to work — simply call and ask, 'How are you feeling?' Then respond with empathy, 'I'm sorry to hear that'. And finish by reaffirming, 'You get some rest, and I will talk to you again (tomorrow, on Friday, next week)'.

In this way, the employee feels that they are genuinely cared about. Remember that, as human beings, our primary emotional need is for connection. Through this very simple conversation, we convey empathy and concern, which stimulates the employee's central nervous system to release endorphins that make them feel calm, and lowers cortisol levels, reducing inflammation and boosting immune system activation, speeding recovery.

How can you innovate for injured workers?

I have operated in this system for many years — on both sides of it. We need to afford workers support when they are injured, but we also need to provide more immersive support in the first three months of their injury. Most insurers and employers might engage a rehabilitation provider to work with the injured worker, but they are not usually appointed fast enough, and they are seen as 'police' by the injured worker. There is no effort in building a relationship, rather the role is driven by KPIs that are geared to getting the injured worker back to work as soon as possible.

This relationship, therefore, doesn't ever make the injured worker feel like it is a support for their recovery, rather they feel like it's an imposition and injured workers see the rehabilitation consultant as working for the employer's interests. Because the relationship is driven by KPIs, the injured worker feels like a commodity.

In thinking about the alternative ways that this could be done to ensure effective outcomes, I was reminded of an anti-recidivism program that was run in Victoria about ten years ago. In essence, it was a well-known fact that people who had been incarcerated were likely to re-offend within three months of being released from prison. The reasons for this essentially revolve around the sense of disconnect that the former inmate has with their community. So this program provided newly released prisoners a case worker, someone who worked with them daily for three months. This person supported them to reconnect with their family, establish them in housing and support them to access local services and create social connections. By providing them support to reconnect with their community, they were able to stay away from the criminal networks, and, therefore, stay out of trouble.

Under the National Disability Insurance Scheme (NDIS) in Australia, we have the ability to engage a 'recovery coach' for a person with disability. The role of the recovery coach is to provide structured support to ensure that the person with disability is able to engage in a wide variety of activities that support their growth and improvement and increase their social engagement. The recovery coach can support their clients to set goals, put in place plans to achieve them and provide the impetus to take action.

In essence, this is what the rehabilitation providers were meant to do, but the remuneration system is too focused on KPIs to get this person into some form of work. They even attend their medical appointments to encourage the doctor to push the person back to work. The focus of the role is all wrong, and their purpose becomes about the employer or the insurer and not about the injured worker. The relationship that is established is an adversarial one, rather than a collegiate one.

So how do we change this?

There are several things that need to be considered, but the best situation would be to use all of the information contained in the first part of this book to ensure that the injured worker remains in the workplace — to recover at work.

If a situation develops where the worker needs to be out of the work environment for an extended period of time due to a physical injury, then a recovery coach should be dispatched to conduct a home or hospital visit within the first three days post injury. The focus of this visit is purely about how the business can support the injured worker to return to the work environment.

If the injury is a psychosocial one, then the same approach needs to be taken — a recovery coach is dispatched to the injured worker's home to develop a comprehensive support plan. Depending on the size of the organisation, this should include an examination of alternative workplace options.

These are opportunities for the employer to intervene early, to prevent an insurance claim from being made.

Workers Compensation Claim done?

What if a workers compensation claim has been lodged? Most employers react like a deer in the headlights to this news, and they take no action for fear that anything that they try will be viewed as further harassment.

I completely understand that fear, because once a medical certificate has been issued, there is some concern that any contact could be perceived as harassment. However, if you establish an expectation that there will be some contact made by the employer, with a view to recovery coaching, then the employee will expect this and understand the intention behind it.

The earlier you can intervene, the better the injured worker's recovery. Most employers feel uncomfortable with taking any action that might make the situation worse, but when you have set the groundwork around the process, the employee expects that you will be in contact. The biggest stumbling block to recovery is inaction!

Now, it's not okay to make contact and harass a person about when they are coming back to work, but the fear around the perception of the contact is what creates the avoidance. Anything that feels like its outside expectations feels uncomfortable, and as human beings we will avoid the discomfort. That is why you need to establish the baseline expectation that you will be in contact, and you do this when you induct the employee into the organisation.

That means that, now that they are off work, you have already established the permission to make contact. You have also already prepared them for what you are going to do by making contact at this time, so when you tell them that you are sending a recovery coach to support them, they feel valued by the provision of support rather than perceiving that they are being spied upon.

The recovery coach should spend at least three hours with them initially, hearing their story and finding out what the injured worker needs to recover. At this stage, the situation may be able to be resolved through mediation. This is to be presented to the injured worker as a wellbeing intervention, designed to support them through a difficult period.

There are many reasons a psychosocial injury may occur, but the majority of them involve inappropriate actions or behaviour by someone in the workplace. If you reflect back on what I outlined in chapter 5 about the difference between action validation and recognition validation, the sole purpose of engaging a recovery coach is to provide recognition validation, and to find a solution that ensures the affected staff member remains in the workplace while they recover.

As you can see, all of these activities are designed to avoid a workers compensation claim being submitted. These are actions that need to be undertaken by a compassionate leader. The larger your organisation, the more likely it is that these activities may be centralised with the human resources area. However, it is essential that the people involved in recovery coaching are able to remain unbiased about the circumstances that led to the injury and focused on supporting the affected worker. There is no room for cynicism in the role of recovery coach.

That may seem like a strange point to make, but it is very common for us to become cynical when we are exposed to similar situations time and again. Like anything, when we are immersed in something we tend to assume that it is everywhere. This is how we develop stigmatising behaviour and 'group think'. It is a well-known phenomenon that mental health professionals are the most stigmatising around mental health! HR managers can believe that employees are just interested in entitlements. Many helping professions can develop cynicism around their client base if they're not careful.

Now the insurer is involved

Once the insurer is involved, it is almost impossible for the employer to intervene in any 'meaningful' way. The employer will need to provide support for any graduated return to work program, depending on the injury. As the employer, it is important to provide as much flexibility as possible for the injured worker, but this has to be balanced with meaningful work.

One of the biggest challenges with graduated return to work programs is the perception around the injured worker's ability to fully contribute. As a result, many employers don't provide the injured worker with 'meaningful' work. Regardless of whether the injury is physical or psychological, the worker needs to be asked what contribution they can make and afforded the opportunity to make it.

Many employers have become so 'risk averse' in regard to injured workers that they prevent the injured worker returning to the work environment until they are 100 per cent recovered. This is especially the case if a worker injures themselves outside of the workplace and they perform a physical role. This approach can actually make an injured worker feel worse about themselves and their situation, which can, in itself, be a triggering event for a mental health issue.

If a worker is unable to engage in their usual working role, employers often find it difficult to think creatively about how the injured worker's skills might be able to be better utilised. It is very common for an injured worker to return to the work environment in a graduated way only to find that their work has been given to someone else who is full time, and so there is a struggle to find anything more than a bit of filing. It is the lack of planning for the graduated return to work that adds to the injured worker's sense of being a burden.

Brainstorm your injured worker's return with them — consider the skills that they can utilise to meaningfully contribute

---

The best option for a graduated return to work is to provide the injured worker with a project that is meaningful but not time critical. The injured worker should be engaged in the brainstorming session about options for this project, rather than just being handed something that feels like an afterthought. If the injury is physical and the worker needs to undertake physical activities, spend some time exploring the physical limitations and ask the employee what they think that they could do.

Employers often feel frustrated with the fact that they have to support an injured worker in the workplace, because they usually just want the job done by someone. Some roles are quite rigid, and some workplaces are limited in the type of work that they do, so many employers find it easier to just find a temporary replacement for a worker for an extended period of time, and don't want the injured worker in the workplace until they feel that they are getting 'full value' from them.

From a business perspective, I completely understand the challenge. There is a cost to the employer in supporting such flexibility, but it's a small cost in comparison to the impact of a workers compensation claim on your premium, in addition to the costs of training new staff. The larger the organisation, the bigger the cost of staff turnover and the less visibility staff turnover has to the bottom line. The larger the organisation, the less personal responsibility staff feel towards the cost of human resources.

This is why it is essential to document the policies and procedures that enable the business to minimise turnover. Once the business grows to more than 10 staff, you need to have a dedicated human resource manager who ensures that your most expensive business assets are well managed and supported — your people.

Can we fix a long term problem?

In this book I have outlined many things that you should do to ensure that you don't create injuries in the workplace, but for some of you, your organisation hasn't managed this well in the past and you may be aware that there are some employees who are disengaged from the work environment and on leave and may have been that way for a long time. How can you help these injured workers? You don't have any of the expectations in place that I have outlined for you, and so there is no basis upon which to initiate engagement with them. In some circumstances, there may be employees who have been off work for several years. So how can you help them?

The first thing to do is to contact them to let them know that you are reviewing your workplace wellbeing programs, and you were hoping to obtain some feedback from them about their experience. This must be a genuine approach that is modelled as an opportunity for improvement. Let them know that this is an opportunity to help improve the policies and procedures, to ensure that their experience can be captured in some 'lessons learned' so that they might help to shape the organisation's approach, in the hope that it will prevent such a situation happening again.

Most people want to find meaning from adversity. Even when they're completely cynical about the motivations behind such an approach, they will usually embrace the opportunity to tell you how badly they were treated. The key to this feedback is to ensure that you are able to steer the conversation to asking them the 'miracle question'. If we could wave a magic wand and this situation had been handled differently for you, what would that have looked like?

Given the opportunity, most injured workers want to feel that their pain and suffering wasn't in vain. As such, they will usually be open to opportunities for things to change. Who knows, it may give rise to providing them an opportunity to contribute to the work environment once again!

Matthew's story

Matthew has been an occupational therapist for 30 years, the majority of which he worked in tertiary rehabilitation as a provider. One area of Matthew's work involved assisting injured workers return to work, and he understands the process of how that works in practice, including the challenges of getting someone back to work.

Matthew joined a workplace health and safety organisation as an investigator. He noticed a growing prevalence of psychosocial injuries, in particular, as a result of workplace bullying. Eventually, he was overseeing an agency that uncovered 55 cases of bullying and harassment, and required seven full-time investigators.

Matthew left his role in the private sector to work in government. After several years there, he identified a serious incident involving corruption. When he escalated the issue to the most senior person in the organisation, who was responsible for security and corruption in government, he was treated like a whistle-blower. His sole focus was to try and save the government a lot of money and public embarrassment.

The policy was clear, but because Matthew escalated the issue outside of his department, he was isolated and excluded by his colleagues, and made to feel like he had done the wrong thing. Matthew continued working, but felt like he was fighting his employer. Eventually, five staff were exposed for fraudulent activity; they had been covering up for each other.

Despite Matthew's report being true, it took three years for the matter to be resolved, and for Matthew to finally feel vindicated. He never felt supported by senior management, even though he was just doing the job that he had been brought in to do.

During that time, Matthew's mental health deteriorated. He was stressed and anxious. Matthew began to develop physical symptoms, such as balance issues, chronic headaches and memory problems, and underwent extensive medical testing to find out what the problem was. Not surprisingly, there started to be questions about his performance. It's quite common for a stressed employee to under-perform, and it added significantly to Matthew's distress.

Senior management used this as an opportunity to remove him from the work environment. They claimed to be concerned for his mental health, but he really felt pushed out. It was a very stressful and high-pressured work environment, yet up until this point, he had really thrived in it. In the end, the specialist came to the conclusion that his symptoms weren't physical, they were psychological. Matthew was diagnosed with a conversion disorder, now called Functional

Neurological Disorder (FND), which causes physical changes to the brain as a result of prolonged exposure to stress. It was at this point that Matthew lodged a workers compensation claim, which was eventually accepted.

Matthew wanted to return to work. He was passionate about his work, but he felt totally devalued. The Independent Medical Examiner recommended he not work in that area again; however, there was no system of support to provide him with an alternative work environment. In the end, Matthew utilised his own networks and found an opportunity in a different work area and began a graduated return-to-work process.

When Matthew was experiencing his greatest challenges, there was no organisational support provided to him. It was only after his claim was accepted that he was provided a rehabilitation provider.

The specialist had indicated that Matthew was never to return to his former work area. That made it challenging for the employer because he was a very senior employee and all he wanted to do was to get back to his role. It didn't help that they didn't understand his FND. They were concerned about putting more stress on him and about their duty of care, but they didn't involve Matthew in the decision-making.

In the end, they found him a role that basically started out with filing. He would regularly be triggered in the new work environment because it involved internal government investigations, so the content would remind him of his own situation. Matthew struggled with memory and balance, but he slowly increased his work hours. It took about six months to get him back to four hours, five days a week, and a further 12 months before he was back working full-time. He still has balance issues and he can be triggered, but he feels valued and capable of making a meaningful contribution.

It was a slow recovery. Matthew had been out of the work environment for 14 months. He needed to be given a supportive working environment, with a network of people who understood that he had an injury and needed to be provided meaningful work with reasonable adjustments.

In the beginning they were not sure what to give him as he was only there for a short period of time, so he was given filing and not much meaningful work. Matthew struggled with the difference in work, but took the approach that he was still being paid and he was aware that he was struggling to focus.

Due to his own rehabilitation background, he tried to stay positive. He was back in the workforce and it provided him a significant mental shift, and an opportunity to reframe in a positive way. As time went on, he began reviewing files, but the nature of the work was similar to his own story, so it was triggering.

Matthew tried to use his experience to afford the individuals affected by his work some compassion and understanding about their situation. In this way, he felt that his experience was affording him some sense of purpose in his work.

For Matthew, this then led to him wanting to see change for other injured workers. He wanted to educate management about the need to understand both sides of a situation and support an injured worker to recover. This gave him some additional passion to improve things for other employees, so that they can avoid the situation he had found himself in.

You need a senior leadership focus on mental health

Many medium-to-large enterprises are adopting a senior leadership focus on mental health and wellbeing. This role is one that is still evolving in many sectors, but it encompasses the oversight of the psychosocial challenges in modern workplaces and seeks to address them with a clear leadership focus.

Chief Mental Health Advisor/Happiness Officer are terms that are growing in popularity as the focus on mental health in the workplace has expanded post pandemic. Despite the name, it's important to ensure that the person who fulfills the role is not just the company 'Agony Aunt'.

It's a tricky space to balance, but depending on the personality, we often see that the HR manager or wellbeing officer becomes the person that everyone complains to. In a toxic work environment, they can become the chief gossip. This person should never become the company counsellor! The responsibility of the role should be to 'triage' personal challenges affecting staff and redirect them to appropriate resources. It's essential that the person that heads up wellbeing is focused on solutions.

The C-Suite head of mental health and wellbeing needs to be focussed on solutions

---

Recipe for Success: The role of the Chief Happiness Officer

The Chief Happiness Officer needs to understand the issues in the organisation and have their finger on the pulse, so they can identify and resolve any issues within the organisation before they escalate. Depending on the size of the organisation, this person is likely to have some background in organisational psychology, rather than HR.

They need to be the strategic thinker around the wellbeing of your people, they are prepared for how any change in the organisation may affect your people, and plan for it. Ideally, they are part of the senior leadership team, involved in the planning of major projects so they can look ahead for potential challenges that any change in the work environment may have for the workers.

A Chief Happiness Officer is constantly looking to the future. They need to be early adopters of technology and prepared to understand how technology may improve the process of your business, and be able to develop effective communication to help your people come on board.

This person needs to be the central hub of communication; they should have exceptional people skills and be able to motivate people. In an idealistic Myers-Briggs world, this person is an ENFP (extroverted, intuitive, feeling, perceptive) because they are empathetic and communicate well. As Myers-Briggs say, the ENFP can find justifiable reasons for anything they want, and influence others to want it too!

There are multiple dimensions to promoting wellness in your business. The Chief Happiness Officer should form part of the corporate/human resources management team. They will keep apprised of the data that monitors the potential hotspots in an organisation by reviewing HR data (see chapter 3 for more on this). They provide insights into wellbeing programs for staff, and act as first point of contact for any staffing incidents, so they can tackle any traumatic incidents within the first six hours, to ensure that the staff member is supported and provided access to resources.

The Chief Happiness Officer should monitor staff satisfaction and workplace culture. They need to put in place clear obligations for leaders around performance output and staff wellbeing, and monitor them. They need to review policies and procedures, and ensure that induction for new employees is completed; they will also monitor the new employee's satisfaction across the first three months of their employment.

They need to develop policies that support psychological safety in the workplace by maintaining oversight of emerging research, and by engaging staff in pilot projects to improve wellbeing. Informal and formal feedback about challenges that staff may be experiencing will enable them to provide a solutions-focussed approach.

Finally, they need a budget and authority to enact change and support the business with resources as required. The Chief Happiness Officer needs to demonstrate empathy and awareness, and mentor the same in the leadership. They need to swiftly address any concerns raised by any member of staff about any issue; they need to develop an early warning system to put out spot fires.

Depending on the size of the organisation, you may require the services of a consulting chief mental health advisor, such as myself, to support a full review of the organisation's current culture and formulate a plan for the implementation of a variety of projects or change programs designed to improve culture. Such a review can define the role of the Chief Happiness Officer for your organisation and recommend the time required for the role.

There are significant benefits to the business in having a dedicated focus on workplace wellbeing and the prevention of psychosocial injuries in the workplace — a role that encourages diversity, embraces flexibility and can find a solution to any perceived conflict in your organisation. In bringing this focus to the fore you will ensure that you are able to tackle trauma, promote psychological safety and boost happiness in your workplace.

Why we need to continuously improve

The ability to really enact change in outcomes for injured workers begins in the workplace. Taking the time to improve your workplace culture, clarify uncertainties in HR policies, and monitor known data to develop an early warning system are essential for preventing psychosocial injuries in the workplace.

Significant improvement in outcomes for injured workers can be achieved through innovation

---

Beginning with recruitment, we need to take the time to understand the personality traits that already exist in the organisation, and what other traits are needed to balance the team. We should improve the recruitment process by looking at several measures of organisational fit, and back this up with interview questions that provide insight into the personality of the potential recruit to assess how they will fit in with the organisational culture.

We want to embed a strong culture of support for new staff, with a comprehensive induction and structured program of support and checking in over the first three months of their employment. This is not just about their performance, but to get a sense of their experience of the workplace while mentoring them to overcome any challenges. This needs to include three-way conversations with their supervisor and other team members, if appropriate.

We need to address interpersonal challenges immediately, and provide recognition validation for our people's experiences — whether we agree with their perspective or not. If there is a disagreement about HR entitlements between a manager and their staff, the HR manager needs to be notified, as it is an early warning indicator of a bigger issue.

Supporting people through challenges

Intervening early whenever a staff member goes on extensive leave, especially if it's stress leave, is essential to their re-engagement. Remember, you are going to set up the expectation for this contact in their onboarding or as part of your change program around improving wellbeing. It's essential that we engage with the staff member as quickly as possible to understand the problem and reassure them of their value, as well as your commitment to finding a solution as soon as possible. Then you are going to follow through.

Providing human resource backup for employees who need to take leave for more than one week for personal reasons, whether the worker has injured themselves inside or outside of work, has a health issue or a family obligation, is also important for supporting internal workplace relations. The business also needs to support the work area to continue to deliver the work without developing resentment towards the absent worker.

We should provide a safe environment to enable a recovery at work program for affected staff. The team leader in this environment needs to be empathic and supportive, and recognise that it will take the employee up to three months to get back to full capacity. This is not a drain on your resources! A workers compensation claim is a major drain on your resources in terms of time under investigation and lost productivity of the team involved in the claims process. It's much better to keep a staff member involved in some level of work output so they remain engaged and feel valued.

You have the tools to be the compassionate leader you want to be

When you picked up this book, you were inspired by the notion that change really is possible. You want to be a compassionate leader. You want to create a safe environment for your people, and you want them to be happy when they are at work — because you care. You probably just didn't know how to go about it.

I hope that through this book you have come to understand why the profitability of your business really is dependent upon providing the right culture for your people. You now understand why our societal changes are making this the most challenging time for businesses in the post-industrial world. Now you have the tools and the guidance to implement positive change in your work and your community. If we all lead with compassion, the world will become a much more balanced space.

I often say to my clients that they are the hero of their journey; I am merely a guide. The hero is the one who needs to take action.

Guidance in the face of inaction is a waste of time and effort for both of us

---

Next Steps: The power of three

There is an interesting phenomenon around the power of three. Whenever we add three elements together, it creates a synergy that is greater than the sum of each element on its own. We also make change in multiples of three, so I want you to set some goals that you want to achieve in your business over the next three weeks, six weeks, three months and six months — significant markers that will help you increase your awareness of your current workplace culture.

Who, what, when, where, why and how

I want to support you to take action, to move forward in your journey to achieving mastery over the mental health of your workplace. Research shows that merely setting a goal is not enough.[48] Your chances of success in achieving your goals are mediated by a number of factors. The probability of success increases with accountability:

- 10 per cent: If you have an *actual* idea or goal (the what).

- 25 per cent: If you *consciously* decide you will do it (the where).

- 40 per cent: If you decide *when* you will do it (the when).

- 50 per cent: If you plan *how* you will do it (the how).

- 65 per cent: If you *commit* to someone, you will do it (the who).

- 95 per cent: If you have a *specific* accountability appointment with a person you've *committed* to (the why).

Find your 'why'

Your journey doesn't end here. In fact, I hope you feel inspired to dive in and start leading consciously. The journey to a balanced workplace has its own ups and downs, which is why I have provided a suite of resources to help you on your travels.

Head over to www.howtohealaworkplace.com, and on the 'Next Steps' page you will find the resources to help you take action and begin to heal your workplace.

I wish you all the best for your journey!

References

1. Safe Work Australia 2022, Mental health overview, Safe Work Australia, viewed 12 August 2022, https://www.safeworkaustralia .gov.au/safety-topic/managing-health-and-safety/mental-health/ psychosocial-hazards.
2. Williams K 2017, 'Toxic Culture: enabling incivility in the U.S. Military and what to do about it', *Joint Force Quarterly*, vol. 87.
3. Ryff, CD & Keyes, CLM 1995, 'The structure of psychological well-being revisited', *Journal of Personality and Social Psychology*, vol. 69, pp. 719-27.
4. Koropets, O 2019, 'Toxic Workplace: problem description and search for management solutions', Kidmore End: European Conference on Management, Leadership & Governance.
5. Gallup Workplace 2021, 'The "Great Resignation" is really the "Great Discontent", Gallup, viewed 12, August 2022, https://www .gallup.com/workplace/351545/great-resignation-really-great-discontent.aspx.
6. U.S. Bureau of Labor Statistics 2022, 'Databases, tables and calculators by subject', U.S. Bureau of Labor Statistics, viewed 12 August 2022, https://data.bls.gov/timeseries/JTS000000000000000QUR.
7. Australian Bureau of Statistics 2022, 'Job mobility', Australian Bureau of Statistics, viewed 12 August 2022, https://www.abs.gov .au/statistics/labour/jobs/job-mobility/latest-release#data-download.

8. Office for National Statistics 2022, LFS: Economically inactive: UK: all: aged 16-64: thousands: SA, Office for National Statistics, viewed 20 August 2022, https://www.ons.gov.uk/employmentand labourmarket/peoplenotinwork/economicinactivity/timeseries/lf2m/lms.

9. Strauss, W & Howe, N 1991, *Generations: The history of America's future, 1584 to 2069*, New York: William Morrow.

10. Mannheim, K 1952, 'The problem of generations', In Kecskemeti P (ed.), *Essays on the sociology of knowledge*, London: Routledge & Kegan Paul.

11. Yano, JM, Yu, K, Donaldson, GP, Shastri, GG, Ann, P, Ma, L, Nagler, CR, Ismagilov, RF, Mazmanian, SK & Hsiao, EY 2015, 'Indigenous bacteria from the gut microbiota regulate host serotonin biosynthesis, Cell, vol. 161, pp. 264-76.

12. Afifi, TD, Zamanzadeh, N, Harrison, K & Callejas, MA 2018, 'WIRED: The impact of media and technology use on stress (cortisol) and inflammation (interleukin IL-6) in fast paced families', *Computers in Human Behavior*, vol. 81, pp. 265-73.

13. Hogan, R, Curphy, GJ & Hogan, J 1994, 'What we know about leadership: Effectiveness and personality', *American Psychologist*, vol. 49, pp. 493-504.

14. George, TJ, Atwater, LE, Maneethai, D, Madera & JM 2022, 'Supporting the productivity and wellbeing of remote workers: Lessons from COVID-19', *Organizational Dynamics*, vol. 51.

15. Bhatia, A & Mohsin, F 2020, 'Comprehensive literature review on workplace happiness linked to employee outcomes', *Test Engineering and Management*, vol. 83, pp. 29266-79.

16. Ross, F, 'Typology', Society of Analytical Psychology, cited 24 June 2022, https://www.thesap.org.uk/articles-on-jungian-psychology-2/about-analysis-and-therapy/typology/.

17. McCormack, MH 1986, *What they don't teach you at Harvard Business School*, Bantam.

18. Gregory, K 2016, 'The importance of employee satisfaction', silo.tips, viewed 12 August 2022, https://silo.tips/download/the-importance-of-employee-satisfaction.

19. Baumeister, RF & Leary, MR 1995, 'The need to belong: desire for interpersonal attachments as a fundamental human motivation', *Psychological Bulletin*, vol. 117, pp. 238-46.

20. Van der Kolk, BA 2014, *The Body Keeps The Score*, London: Allen Lane.

21. Logie, R, Bowers, M, Dent, A, Elliott, J, O'Connor, M & Russell A 2020, *Using Stories in EMDR*, Hove: Trauma Aid UK.

22. Howe, ML & Courage, ML 1997, 'The emergence and early development of autobiographical memory', *Psychological Review*, vol. 104, pp. 499-523.

23. Nelson, K & Fivush, R 2004, 'The emegence of autobiographical memory: a social cultural developmental theory', *Psychological Review*, vol. 111, pp. 486-511.

24. Siegel, DJ 2015, *The developing mind: How relationships and the brain interact to shape who we are*, New York: Guilford Publications.

25. McAdams DP 2001, 'The psychology of life stories', *Review of General Psychology*, vol. 5, pp. 100-22.

26. Ochoa, P, Lepeley, M-T & Essens, P 2019, *Wellbeing for Sustainability in the Global Workplace*, London: Routledge.

27. Beyond Blue 2018. 'Answering the call - national survey. National Mental Health and Wellbeing Study of Police and Emergency Services - Final Report', Melbourne: Beyond Blue Ltd, p. 126.

28. Howard, KA, Griffiths, KM, McKetin, R & Ma, J 2018. 'Can a brief biologically-based psychoeducational intervention reduce stigma and increase help-seeking intentions for depression in young people? A randomised controlled trial', *Journal of Child & Adolescent Mental Health*, vol. 30, no. 1.

29. Fernandez-Stark, K, Couto, V & Bamber, P 2019, 'Industry 4.0 in developing countries: the mine of the future and the role of women', World Bank Group, p. 34.

30. Minerals Council of South Africa 2020, 'In the spotlight: women in mining in South Africa', Minerals Council of South Africa, viewed 18 September 2022, https://www.mineralscouncil.org.za/special-features/1064-women-in-mining-in-south-africa.

31. Peterson, SJ & Bartels, AL 2017, 'Using neuroscience methods to explore gender differences in leadership', in SR Madsen (ed), *Handbook of research on gender and leadership*, Cheltenham: Edward Elgar Publishing, pp. 238-.

32. Lerner, JS & Keltner, D 2001, 'Fear, anger and risk', *Journal of Personality & Social Psychology*, vol. 81, pp. 146-59.

33. Gur, RC, Gunning-Dixon, F, Bilker, WB & Gur, RE 2002, 'Sex differences in temporo-limbic and frontal brain volumes of healthy adults', *Cerebral Cortex*, vol. 12, pp. 998-1003.

34. Google 2021, 'Diversity', viewed 31 October 2022, https://diversity.google/annual-report/static/pdfs/google_2021_diversity_annual_report.pdf.

35. Parker, M 2022, 'Google - The Keyword', viewed 31 October 2022, https://blog.google/outreach-initiatives/diversity/diversity-annual-report-2022.

36. Silicon Valley Bank, 2019, 'Half of startups have no women on their leadership team | Silicon Valley Bank', viewed 31 October 2022, https://www.svb.com/trends-insights/reports/women-in-technology-2019.

37. Deci, E & Ryan, R 2017, *Self-determination theory: basic psychological needs in motivation, development, and wellness,* New York: The Guilford Press.

38. Cherr, K 2021, 'Self-determination theory and motivation', viewed 25 June 2022, https://www.verywellmind.com/what-is-self-determination-theory-2795387#:~:text=In%20psychology%2C%20self%2Ddetermination%20is,over%20their%20choices%20and%20lives.

39. Strunin, L & Boden, LI 2004, 'The workers' compensation system: worker friend or foe?', *American Journal of Industrial Medicine*, vol. 45, pp. 338-45.

40. Solender, EK 1993, 'New Zealand's no-fault accident compensation scheme has some unintended consequences: a caution to U.S. reformers', *The International Lawyer*, vol. 27.

41. Miller, JM 1998, 'Compensation for mental trauma injuries in New Zealand', *The Australasian Journal of Disaster and Trauma*

Studies, vol. 3.; ACC v E [1992] 2 NZLR 426,.434. Published by the Ministry of Justice © Crown Copyright. Licensed from the Ministry of Justice for use under the creative commons attribution license (BY) 4.0, according to Copyright | New Zealand Ministry of Justice.

42. Fronsko, A & Woodroffe, A 2017, 'Public vs. private underwriting and administration of personal injury statutory insurance schemes'. Sydney: Institute of Actuaries of Australia, pp. 1-60.

43. Australian Securities and Investments Commission n.d., 'Whistleblower protections', *ASIC*, viewed August 17, 2022, https://asic.gov.au/about-asic/contact-us/how-to-complain/whistleblower-protections/.

44. Perry, J 2019, Application for judicial review: Howard and Comcare (Compensation) [2017] AATA 2381. ACD 96 of 2017, Paragraph 35. Howard v Comcare [2019] FCA 1031 : Federal Court of Australia, July 2, 2019.

45. Tracy, DK & Rix, KJB 2017, 'Malingering mental disorders: clinical assessment', *BJPsych Advances*, vol. 23, pp. 27-35.

46. Cooper, DA, Slaughter, JE & Gilliland, S 2021, 'Reducing injuries, malingering, and workers' compensation costs by implementing overt integrity testing', *Journal of Business and Psychology*, vol. 36, pp. 495-512.

47. Prabook n.d., Loren J Chapman, Prabook, viewed 18 September 2022, https://prabook.com/web/loren_j.chapman/1700011.

48. Phillips, PP 2010, *ASTD Handbook for Measuring and Evaluating Training*, American Society for Training and Development.

Printed and bound by CPI Group (UK) Ltd, Croydon, CR0 4YY

26/11/2024

14600142-0002